HAPPY
WORK

HAPPY WORK

WHY YOUR ORGANIZATION NEEDS TO CREATE A CULTURE OF **HAPPINESS**

NICHOLAS J. WEBB

GOLEADERLOGIC.COM

Any internet addresses, phone numbers, or company or product information
printed in this book are offered as a resource and are not intended in any way
to be or to imply an endorsement by the author, nor does the author vouch for
the existence, content, or services of these sites, phone numbers, companies, or
products beyond the life of this book.

Hatepoints™, Lovepoints™, Happiness as a Service™ (HaaS™), Learnlogic®,
Leaderlogic®, RealRatings™, and RealRating™ are service products of
Leaderlogic, LLC.

Printed in the United States of America

ISBN 978-0-578-34592-5

First Printing

For general information, contact us at www.goleaderlogic.com.
To contact the author, visit www.nickwebb.com.

I would like to dedicate this book to my amazing family:
my wife, Michelle, and our children, Taylor, Madison, Chase, and Paige.

I'd also like to dedicate this work to all the amazing researchers
and clients who have taught me the importance of
a Happy Work culture and, most important, how to achieve it.

Contents

Preface

For over thirty years, I've been honored to serve some of the best brands in the world as a consultant and strategic advisor. During that time, I've seen highly respected CEOs, leaders, and managers launch, with the very best of intentions, "quality of work life" initiatives. These leaders rightly believed that happy employees were better employees, and they sought to make changes that would fulfill those conditions. Regrettably, despite their high expectations, these programs nearly always failed. The metrics they were designed to improve—productivity, employee engagement, and even company profitability—didn't budge. It was as if nothing had been done.

My consulting firm has become something of an organizational hazmat team, tasked with cleaning up after yet another ineffective quality of work life initiative. But failure is the best teacher, and over time, based on my experience with these organizations, I've formulated powerful solutions that really work. The lessons I've learned are presented in the pages of this book. I'll share with you how to avoid the common pitfalls and how to leverage new best practices that provide predictable, measurable returns on your happiness initiative. You will also discover the corollary between happy customers, sales growth, and innovation in the furtherance of happy employees.

I will share with you why you should avoid the vast survey industry, and how to get real insights about what your employees want and need in order to build a workplace that your competitors will envy. Your newly forged happiness initiative will attract and keep the best talent in your marketplace, drive the best innovations, build scalable and predictable revenue growth, and significantly improve the returns on your organizational strategies.

This book contains both deep research and thirty years of practical experience. It is my sincere hope that you will leverage these insights to avoid the common mistakes and enjoy the benefits of proven methods that deliver real results. If applied properly with the correct infrastructure and training, your organization will achieve some or all of the following benefits:

- Attracting and keeping the best talent in your market
- Significant increases in employee productivity and presentism
- Reduced workforce stress and healthcare costs
- Improved returns on enterprise strategy
- Major improvements in customer experience
- Predictable and measurable increases in revenue
- Improvements and cost reduction and efficiency
- Predictable improvements and innovation

We live in challenging times. All over the world, employees of companies large and small are questioning their career choices. Instead of taking their life path for granted and settling for what society offers them, many are asking, "Is this all there is? Why should I commute to a boring or distasteful job with little future, just to pay my mortgage? I want to do something that has meaning to me. I want to get up and go to work with a smile on my face."

The Great Resignation served as a wake-up call. Today, the best companies have to compete for the best employees, and it's not just about the size of the paycheck, it's about performing meaningful work that creates value. I wrote this book to give every company—*your* company—a road map to relevance and competitiveness, and to help make Happy Work a reality.

Introduction

The title of this book unites two words that have not been seen together often enough: "happy" and "work."

Happy means the full range of positive human emotions, from transitory, visible happiness—a smile and a laugh—to the much deeper and long-lasting sense of self-satisfaction that comes from helping others live better lives.

Work is the activity that produces value for society and provides the means of support for the person doing the work.

For centuries, these two concepts were unrelated. Work was serious, happiness was frivolous. Work was difficult, happiness was easy. As *Happy Work* will reveal, those days are over. A new day is dawning.

The workplace of today—and tomorrow—looks and feels very different from the workplaces of yesterday. It's no longer about breaking your back for a paycheck. It's not about "putting in your time"—twenty or thirty years—at a job you may not like just for the reward of a gold watch and a pension plan. Today's employees are increasingly independent and focused on their quality of life during every hour of the day, including the hours spent at work. They want to be happy not only at home but at work.

This puts a special responsibility, and opportunity, on the shoulders of business leaders. This is because within any organization, the happiness of employees is shaped by the CEO and his or her top leadership. Sadly, too few leaders recognize this, and consequently they're open to significant risk. In a typical, poorly directed organization, leaders are not concerned with the emotional state of individual workers and managers. As long as the employees show up and do their jobs, they can be randomly happy or unhappy. The leader does not care which. This neglect makes the employees subject to both internal and external pressures, and if an employee happens to be happy today, he or she might be unhappy tomorrow.

Such volatility impedes sustainable progress. Unhappy workers are corrosive, eating away at the framework of the company until it's crippled. Unhappy workers are difficult to salvage. If you ask them if there's a problem, they will nearly always point to some other irritation in their lives. They'll never say, "Yes—the problem is with me! I'm miserable in my job." Instead, they'll say it was so-and-so's fault, or the customers aren't buying, or the marketing wasn't effective. Such responses send leaders on a wild-goose chase, wasting time and resources trying to solve problems that may not exist.

In contrast, the leaders of a happy company make a long-term effort to nurture a consistent culture of positivity. They know the happiness of their employees—indeed, of all their stakeholders at every level—holds the key to sustained success and robust profits. For that reason, they make happiness an institutional priority, and if they get it right, they know that everything else—R&D, marketing, human resources, operations, finance, and profitability—will come along the same positive path.

From Cradle to Grave

Happy Work begins by tracing the history and meaning of being happy at work. During America's great industrial expansion that began in the early nineteenth century, employee happiness mattered very little. Our collective journey from an agrarian society to a manufacturing and technology powerhouse meant that companies were in the driver's seat, so to speak. The goal was to make America globally dominant, and through two world wars we managed to do exactly that. The question of workplace happiness was irrelevant. But at the same time, between big companies and labor there was a tacit agreement: In return for compliance and minimal concern about employee happiness, many firms offered lifetime employment, or something close to it. An employee could imagine working for the same company for their entire career before retiring with a comfortable pension. If they suffered along the way, no harm done, because in the end they got their reward.

In the middle of the twentieth century, IBM represented the apex of how companies treated workers and thought of their roles in society. Its culture was called "cradle to grave," meaning if you got in, they'd take care of you. Thomas Watson Sr., and his son, Thomas Watson Jr., who together ran the company during this time, articulated three values for the company, one of which was "respect for the individual." With it came one of the most astonishing policies in American business history: "As businessmen," said Watson Jr., "we think in terms of profits, but people continue to rank first."

For more than seven decades, IBM never laid off workers. If the business hit a slump, then workers might be retrained and relocated. To distribute labor where it was needed, workers were simply transferred to different locations across the country or even overseas, giving IBM the internal moniker, "I've Been Moved."

While a worker may not have been terribly happy at his day-to-day job, he could feel a deeper sense of happiness knowing that his efforts were supported by loyalty from his employer.

We know what happened to that ethos. Hammered by overseas competition, in 1993 IBM did the unthinkable: it laid off 60,000 workers. By the dawn of the twenty-first century, across every industry respect for the individual had been replaced by a relentless drive toward "shareholder value." Employees were suddenly faced with the worst of both worlds: Companies that cared neither about their happiness nor their loyalty. The poster child for the new corporate attitude was General Motors, whose disregard for both customers and employees led to declining quality, slumping sales, and ultimately, in 2009, bankruptcy.

As America emerged from the Great Recession, the national marketplace saw seismic changes, and the consumer emerged with greater power than ever. Thanks to the digital revolution and the dawning of the

Information Age, the balance of power shifted from companies to their customers. The accelerating pace of innovation brought new pressure on companies to meet the high expectations of the marketplace. Consumers could research products online and then buy at the cheapest price. If the company performed poorly, the consumer could post a negative review for all the world to see.

Meanwhile, betrayed by employers who treated them as cost centers, employees felt no loyalty, and without hesitation hopped from one job to a better one. Companies responded by routinely demanding noncompete clauses in employment contracts. But the pendulum kept swinging, and consumers, shareholders, and employees alike began to demand that companies become socially responsible and get back to the old idea of "respect for the individual"—with those individuals being employees, customers, and even people who lived where the company did business.

As we plunge deeper into the twenty-first century, employees and consumers alike have begun to demand that as long as we have mega-corporations that are fickle in their behavior, then the least they can do is foster a sense of happiness.

Happy Workers = Money in the Bank

In the pages ahead, the book will reveal the ascendent power of the happy worker, and how savvy business owners must harness it for greater market dominance and profits. While some shortsighted companies resist this disruption, organizations with their eyes on the future realize that happy workers have the power to both lower risk and increase reward.

For two big reasons, cultivating a happy workplace is like putting money in the bank.

Happy workers reduce bad things. Workforce happiness lowers healthcare costs, absenteeism, employee actions against the employer, employee theft, and the power wielded by disgruntled employees and the nasty stuff they'll post online. It reduces customer complaints about poor service and minimizes foreseeable, avoidable accidents and slowdowns due to employee disengagement.

Happy workers make good things happen. They significantly improve employee recruitment and onboarding, boost employee productivity and return on human capital investment, and heighten engagement that drives more safety and higher quality.

The book will examine the impact of the Covid-19 economy on the relationship of workers to their employers, and how workers who were happy before the pandemic were much more likely to stick around during and after, while workers who were unhappy before the pandemic, and who were not treated well during it, were much more likely to quit. This pattern serves notice to employers who are getting away with disrespecting employees when times are good that if disruption comes—which it will eventually in some form—then those employees will be the first to head for the exits.

It will reveal how workplace happiness can result in major reductions in employee healthcare costs, as well as significant cost savings in recruitment and employee onboarding due to higher employee retention rates. It allows you to attract mission-critical talent and is fundamental to driving inclusion and equity. In terms of increased productivity, happy workplaces see a higher return on human capital, improved sustainable innovation, and more powerful delivery of market-leading customer experiences.

For your brand, the happy workplace will reduce revenue loss from derogatory online ratings and build your reputational value.

Practical Steps You Can Take

Happy Work shows you that change is impossible without the sincere and fulsome endorsement of the organizational leadership. Leaders must recognize that progress takes time. If you take one small step every day for a year, you will get much farther than if you took one giant leap and then stopped. Incremental improvement is the way to get it done!

Shortsighted leaders see a focus on employee happiness as an *expense*. Low wages, harsh working conditions, and a strictly top-down command structure may cost less in the short term, but if you want meaningful, sustained growth and success, you should be willing to make the necessary *investment*. It's no different from investing in new equipment, job training, or research and development. You expect to see a return on your investment, and you will.

This is not a book of theory. *Happy Work* reveals, step by step, the actions you can take *starting today* that will strengthen your employee morale and give you positive results. It begins by showing you how happy employees—and their close cousins, happy customers and other stakeholders—can make a measurable difference in the profitability of your company. Having taken care of that piece of business, the book tackles the most vexing question facing many well-intentioned leaders: How do you define a happy employee? And having formulated a definition, how do you then determine if your employees are truly happy?

It introduces the Happy Work formula:

$$\text{Work} + \text{Recreation} + \text{Meaning} = \text{Happy Work}$$

If you can craft a company culture that strikes a balance between those three components—work, recreation, and meaning—then you've taken a big step toward creating a happy and satisfying work environment.

In our modern world, surveys have become ubiquitous. They have become the tool of choice for discerning the emotional temperature of groups of people, including employees. Here's the problem: We all know that ordinary employee surveys are often flawed or misleading. They either ask the wrong questions or they allow employees to paint a false picture. This is why *Happy Work* offers an innovative new solution—the RealRatings™ system. This transformative survey takes the bold step of not only asking your employees what they like about their work, but also what they specifically *dislike* about it. Let's face it: While it may make you cringe, knowing what your employees hate gives you a very specific problem to solve and can be more useful than knowing what they love.

When administered to a wide cross-section of employees with their various personalities and expectations, one-size-fits-all surveys are doomed to fail. The book shows you how to understand the various archetypes of your employees so that you can survey them more effectively. (Hint: the archetypes have nothing to do with age or gender. You can forget all that malarkey about Millennials versus Boomers!)

While it's important to treat your current employees with respect and help them be happy at work, it's equally important to hire people who you know have the best chance of being happy on the job from day one. The book will show you how to create powerful *employee personas* that will help you—without bias or prejudice—find just the right person for each job.

And for each happy employee there should be a happy job, which helps them contribute to the success of the organization. The book shows you the importance of designing the happy job and how to do it. Here, the emphasis is on "meaning"—the deep personal satisfaction we get when we make something or provide a service that contributes to our culture or improves the lives of others. The happy job needs to be consistent throughout the employee's touchpoint journey from the pre-touch (before they even apply for a position) all the way through the years to the post-retirement touch—which, as we've seen in the after-Covid (or Covid-19) economy, can be more significant than many leaders might think.

The book ends with a handy, practical "Leader's Guide to Making Workplace Happiness Real," which provides a checklist of steps any leader can take to unlock the powerful benefits of a happy workplace.

Ready? Let's get started!

CHAPTER 1

High Ho, High Ho, It's Off to Work We Go!

Have you ever wondered who built the Great Pyramids of Egypt?

Or more precisely, how the workers *felt* as they toiled in the sweltering desert nearly five millennia ago?

Even today, in our era of incredible skyscrapers, the pyramids along the Nile remain astonishing human achievements. The biggest one, the Great Pyramid of Giza, was built around 2600 BCE, and for the next 3,900 years was the tallest man-made structure in the world. (It was knocked off the top spot by the Lincoln Cathedral in the year 1311.) The very first of the Seven Wonders of the Ancient World was constructed using roughly 2.3 million huge blocks of stone, mostly local limestone but also imported white limestone and granite, hauled down the Nile on barges. The army of workers who quarried, shaped, and piled up these stones had no power tools, no cranes, no steel chisels, and no wheeled vehicles.

As a building project, it must have been enormously complex to organize and manage. It was such a massive undertaking that later commentators, who had little knowledge of everyday life in ancient Egypt, assumed the people who did the work had to be slaves. The idea that forced laborers built the pyramids was introduced by the ancient Greek historian Herodotus, who wrote in the fifth century BCE (more than 2,000 years after the fact!) that since the Great Pyramid was built by Khufu, an allegedly tyrannical pharaoh, the workers must have been compelled by force to show up and wrestle the giant stones.

In short, he concluded that the Great Pyramid of Giza was a profoundly *unhappy* worksite—and yet the structure was successfully completed.

This idea took root and became a part of common lore. In the modern era, the notion of a miserable, unhappy slave class in Egypt was popularized by Hollywood productions like Cecil B. De Mille's *The Ten Commandments*, in which captive people labored under the scorching sun, suffering under the lash of pharaoh's cruel overseers. This image dovetailed nicely with the Industrial Revolution's worst excesses, which saw factory owners treat workers more or less like beasts of burden. The idea was that by giving someone a job, no matter how inhumane the conditions, the employer was doing the worker a favor. Unskilled workers were inherently lazy—which is why they were poor—and would only be productive if forced to work.

Across many industries, we've inherited this "taskmaster" mindset that asserts workers at all levels—from executives to burger flippers—must be spurred on by *fear*. This approach says that if left to their own devices, most people would rather sit on the sofa and watch television than dedicate themselves to hard work. To get up and become productive, they need more stick than carrot. The threat of a painful outcome—unemployment, eviction from their house, a life of poverty—is what drives them forward. Sure, there are outliers; people like Jeff Bezos are held up as the exceptions that prove the rule. They are the self-motivated "job creators" who take the unruly and undisciplined entry-level workers and whip them into shape.

Under such a belief system, if a worker is *happy*, then something's wrong. People who are working hard and being productive should not be happy. In fact, they should be the opposite. They should be, well, miserable. Or at least fearful. If they're unsmiling, then the employer knows he's getting the most out of them. No slackers on the job!

To go back to ancient Egypt, it turns out that the picture of workers being forced by the pain of the lash to build an astonishing structure is totally wrong. How do we know this? Since the 1990s, archeologists have been unearthing a sprawling complex—a small city, really—adjacent to the pyramids. The site is called Heit el-Ghurab, and evidence suggests the workers who built the pyramids—roughly 10,000 at any given time over a period of 30 years—lived very well. Archaeologists have uncovered extensive remains from the many belly-filling meals they ate, and animal bones show they received the best cuts of meat, including generous quantities of cattle, goat, sheep, and fish. Hundreds of thousands of bread jars have been found, enough to feed all the workers, who slept in long, purpose-built dormitories. An official record has been found showing that every day during construction, farmers in the Delta and Upper Egypt sent 21 buffalo and 23 sheep to the building site to feed the hardworking builders. These farmers were exempted from paying taxes to the government, suggesting they were willingly participating in a national project.

Ancient graffiti reveals the workers gave their teams nicknames including "the Drunkards of Menkaure" and "the Followers of the Powerful White Crown of Khufu," both referring to names of contemporary pharaohs.

Slaves would never have been treated this well. The workers were probably farmers recruited in the off-season—possibly during Akhet, or the annual Season of the Inundation, during which the Nile flooded and farmland was covered in water. The pyramids were a vast public works project that represented a win-win for everyone. The pharaoh got his gigantic tomb and thousands of workers got good-paying jobs while their farms were awash in river water.

This emerging evidence allows us to blow up the old notion of the rank-and-file builders of the pyramids as slaves driven by the lash. They were almost certainly *happy workers* who enjoyed the two most important things to any worker: being engaged in a meaningful endeavor and receiving good compensation for their efforts.

Thousands of years later, their astonishing work still stands. Not many people can say that!

Work + Recreation + Meaning = Happy Work

Let's start with the question, "Why do we work?"

This may seem like a silly inquiry, but it's actually quite complex and difficult to answer.

On one hand, the response is obvious: we work because we need to put a roof over our head and food on the table. In this case, we define work as an activity that requires effort and produces something of value that can be used or shared.

In contrast, recreation, while it may require effort, is not regarded as producing something of value that can be used or shared.

Manufacturing golf clubs is work.

Using those golf clubs to play eighteen holes is recreation.

Painting a house to protect it from the elements is work.

Painting a picture of a house and tacking it up on your refrigerator is recreation.

Recreation, by definition, is an activity you do *because it makes you happy*. If it didn't make you happy, you wouldn't do it. No one ever played golf because it made them unhappy (except when their ball went straight into the water hazard). No one ever put brush to canvas to paint a picture because the activity made them unhappy.

But it gets more complicated than that. Human beings are perhaps unique in the animal kingdom because we *seek out work* even when we don't have to do it. We like doing work, or at least the work we enjoy. Many humans keep working long past retirement age, even though they already have plenty of money. Perhaps the most well-known example of the perennial worker is Warren Buffett. As of this writing, he's well north of 90 years old. With a net worth of over $100 billion, he could have retired decades ago. But he still shows up every day at the office, and he still does the work he's been doing since he began his career in 1951. Why? Because he enjoys it. It makes him feel good. And by the way, he does take time off for recreation: He's an avid bridge player.

"I play a lot," Buffett told Thomas Heath of the *Washington Post* in a 2017 interview. "At least four sessions a week, about two hours a session." That's a minimum of eight hours a week.[1]

You don't have to be a billionaire to want to keep working. Loren Wade worked as a Walmart greeter well past his 100th birthday. Betty Reid Soskin took a job as a US Park Ranger when she was in her eighties, becoming the nation's oldest. Kenneth Curzon ran the parking services at Scripps Memorial Hospital in La Jolla, California, in his nineties. The list goes on.

Clearly, there must be an intersection between recreation—an activity we do because it makes us happy—and work, which we must do to stay alive.

You could draw a Venn diagram with two circles, work and recreation. The area in the middle, where they intersect, is the area of Happy Work.

It gets even more complicated! Humans often get more out of work than just physical sustenance and if it intersects with recreation, pleasure. There can be a third benefit to work. This is the deep personal satisfaction we get when we make something that contributes to our culture or improves the lives of others. We can call this *meaning*. As Stephen Hawking said, "Work gives you meaning and purpose, and life is empty without it."

The people who built the Great Pyramid of Giza were driven by the feeling they were not just providing sustenance for themselves in terms of being paid but were building a structure that had tremendous significance both to themselves and to their culture. No doubt it was not difficult to recruit workers to the project precisely because the cause was noble and uplifting. This is one reason why people serve in the Army or become park rangers—they feel as though they're serving a cause bigger than themselves.

Work + recreation + meaning = Happy Work.

But just because you work doesn't mean you will feel fulfilled, and how you feel about your work does not necessarily correlate to how much money you make. As John Ruskin said, "Better the rudest work that tells a story or records a fact, than the richest without meaning."

Whether or not your work has meaning to you depends on your point of view. For example, consider two fast-food workers at McDonald's. Both earn minimum wage.

Jane thinks her job as a burger flipper is demeaning and nothing but a short-term way to make some cash. She doesn't care about her customers or their satisfaction. Because she sees her work as essentially meaningless, Jane is an unhappy worker.

Meanwhile, Sally flips burgers too, but she sees her work as providing low-cost, convenient meals for people who are in a hurry or on a budget. She sees the families who come to McDonald's with little kids and how excited they get. She sees the low-income person for whom McDonald's is an affordable meal. Because her work has meaning to her, Sally is a happy worker.

This example is incredibly important because it illustrates the level of employee happiness can vary considerably across equivalent jobs. That leads us to the conclusion—which is the theme of this book—that employers have tremendous influence on how their own employees approach their work. If you have two burger flippers, and one hates her job while the other loves it, you must conclude that if the employer of the job-hater made an effort to reach out to that employee and educate her about the value of her job, she could find happiness in her work.

Happy Work Is Found in Unlikely Places

It's worthwhile to dig a little deeper into the idea that the work you do could satisfy the formula of work + recreation + meaning = Happy Work.

Contrary to popular belief, current research suggests the people who built the Great Pyramid of Giza—which was probably as grueling a job as you'd ever want—were engaged in happy work. We know their work had tremendous meaning to them, and if you interpret "recreation" to mean "feeling good and being well treated," then the three-decades-long project qualified as happy work.

Let's look at the closest analogy we have to the Egyptian pyramid builders: the present-day, all-volunteer U.S. Army. It's a big employer. In fiscal year 2020, the end strength for the Regular Army (USA) was 480,893 soldiers. When you add the Army National Guard (ARNG) and the U.S. Army Reserve (USAR), the combined-component strength of the U.S. Army was 1,005,725 soldiers. That put it at number three, behind Walmart (1.6 million) and Amazon (1.3 million). The pay is almost ludicrously low—the average annual Army salary for a private is just $21,420 a year, plus allowances and other benefits. A staff sergeant with eight years' experience makes only $45,151 a year. Even officer pay is low—a major with eight years' experience makes only $86,306.[2]

Remember, this is for a role in which the job description includes leaving your family, being shipped off to some distant base, and the possibility of going into combat and getting killed or wounded.

In contrast, annual compensation at Walmart ranges from $13,000 for a "service associate" to $157,000 for a senior engineering manager.[3]

At Amazon, the median worker made $29,007 in 2020.[4] Amazon workers are notoriously unhappy—prior to the pandemic, fulfillment centers had an average employee turnover rate of 150 percent per year. Think about that. It means the average employee quit after less than a year on the job. The situation got so bad that Amazon was running out of people to hire and in September 2021 was forced to boost its starting pay to $18 an hour.

Getting back to the Army, you'd think that with the low pay, significant personal and family commitment, and high level of risk, that soldiers would have low levels of job happiness. To be fair, the Army doesn't release statistics about the happiness of its enlisted personnel, but they do share reports about the roughly 188,000 civilian employees.

As the Army News Service reported, in fiscal year 2020 the Army achieved its best overall ratings ever in the Federal Employee Viewpoint Survey. The service posted a civilian employee engagement index rate of 72.7 percent, up three percentage points from the previous year, and saw its biggest increase in the "leaders lead" category, which at 62.7 percent reported a 3.5 percent increase from 2019.

The Army also had an increase in its global satisfaction index to 69 percent. This category measures federal employees' overall satisfaction with their job, pay, and organization. About 70 percent of Army civilians said that they would recommend their organization to others, up from 68 percent the previous year.

"Those are very, very, very good numbers across government [organizations], but exceptional in large organizations," said Todd Fore, deputy assistant secretary of the Army for civilian personnel. "I think it is incredible that we have such a high response rate across the department."[5]

Army uniformed personnel can, and do, post their personal job satisfaction scores on Glassdoor. The Army has hundreds of jobs, and according to WeAreTheMighty.com, the jobs that get the highest scores are often the most dangerous. At the top of the list for Army job happiness are human resource specialists—a nice safe desk job. But at number two comes psychological operations, followed by artillerymen (shooting those big guns), combat engineers (defusing bombs—very dangerous!), communications engineers, Army pilots, and cavalry (tanks and such).[6]

And here's the bottom line: Do uniformed Army personnel choose to reenlist after their period of service is over? Perhaps astonishingly, the answer is yes. In fiscal 2018, the Army accomplished the highest reenlistment rate in its history by achieving a 92 percent rate without lowering any standard. Compare that to Amazon: The Army had an 8 percent quit rate over multiple years versus 150 percent over just one year for Amazon.

"Retention rates being so high tells us many things," said Sgt. Maj. Mark Thompson, a senior Army career counselor. "Mainly that soldiers are happy with their jobs and serving their country. We understand that soldiers talk with their feet. If they're happy, they stay. If they're unhappy, they leave. The great news is, soldiers are choosing to stay in record numbers."[7]

Why do so many men and women volunteer to join an organization that offers low pay, tough working conditions, and personal risk? Because the organization offers many other benefits that humans value highly, including a sense of life purpose, comradery, skills training, and the satisfaction of doing something valued by society. And for many recruits, the Army fulfills a long-standing tradition: the opportunity to get out of town, make a fresh start, get an education, and come out on the other side with a solid platform for living.

And that makes them happy.

The Scrooge Mentality

Despite what may seem to be an obvious truth—that people who enjoy their work perform better at it—the fact is that for much of human history, employers have believed that misery is the most powerful motivator of their workers. Specifically, they've invested themselves in two ideas:

1. Employees who are working hard should not appear to be happy. If they look happy, they're not working hard enough.
2. Employees are like any other component of the supply chain. You want to pay them as little as possible while making them as productive as possible. (We'll see later in the book just how contradictory this formula is.) By definition, this does not produce happiness.

You can call this the Scrooge mentality, in honor of the famous character from *A Christmas Carol* by Charles Dickens. His employee, Bob Cratchit, labors under dreary conditions, in "a dismal little cell," warmed only by the weak heat from one lump of coal. Scrooge himself rails against any thought of creature comforts; he lives only to make money. His cold heart warms only when he's in his counting room. Nothing else matters.

In the world of academia, where people of action often go to find intellectual justification for their personal beliefs, the twentieth century Scrooges of the world found validation in the writings of Milton Friedman. His views roared into the public spotlight on September 13, 1970, when he published an article in the *New York Times*. Rather grandiosely entitled, "A Friedman Doctrine—the Social Responsibility of Business Is to Increase Its Profits," the article asserted, "a corporate executive is an employee of the owners of the business. He has direct responsibility to his employers. That responsibility is to conduct the business in accordance with their desires, which generally will be to make as much money as possible while conforming to the basic rules of the society, both those embodied in law and those embodied in ethical custom."

Friedman's article was adamant: business executives who pursued a goal other than maximizing investor profits were, he said, "unwitting puppets of the intellectual forces that have been undermining the basis of a free society these past decades." They were guilty of "analytical looseness and lack of rigor," and were posing as "unelected government officials" who were illegally taxing employers and customers.

On the surface, you'd think that Friedman and Scrooge would make perfect bedfellows. In the Friedman doctrine, employees are no better than machines to be operated at the lowest possible cost. But Friedman blinked. He slipped in a very interesting caveat when he wrote, "It may well be in the long-run interest of a corporation that is a major employer in a small community to devote resources to providing amenities to that community or to improving its government. That may make it easier to attract desirable employees, it may reduce the wage bill or lessen losses from pilferage and sabotage or have other worthwhile effects. . . ."[8]

Those two sentences hint at what we now know to be true: Organizations that see the big picture and embrace the fact that all of us— owners, employees, customers, investors—are human beings, not robots, will in the long run enjoy higher profits and stronger growth. It can be worthwhile to make an investment in the organization, its employees, and the community, which, by improving overall working conditions, will boost productivity, improve marketing, reduce waste, and result in *higher* profits than if the investment had never been made.

Employees are driven as much by emotion as they are by logic. They work not only for the paycheck but for themselves and the good feeling they get from doing a job they enjoy, and which allows them to go home each night with a feeling of satisfaction.

Take Action!

- ✓ Take some time to think about what makes *you* happy in your work as a leader. Are you engaged in work that makes a difference to your community? Do you feel appreciated and fairly compensated? What would you change if you could?
- ✓ Now think about the people you manage. Given the culture of your organization, can they feel the same sense of satisfaction as you do?
- ✓ Look at the statistics for employee engagement metrics including average tenure, sick days taken, productivity, accidents, and inventory shrinkage. Are they as good as they could be? It's possible that unless your workplace is truly a happy one, you're leaving money on the table.

CHAPTER 2

The Changing World of Work

Human culture is changing more dramatically and at a higher rate than ever before in our history. The pace of innovation and disruption is steadily increasing. Change has become the norm—which means that it's no longer "change" as we used to define it.

Think about the Egyptians who built the Great Pyramid of Giza. That was roughly 5,000 years ago. Think about how they lived their lives, how they communicated, and how they ate and worked. Then fast-forward over 3,000 years to the time of Cleopatra, who died in 30 BCE. How much had changed over three millennia? Very little! Cleopatra's world had some new technologies such as iron tools and wheeled vehicles, but if you transported an ancient Egyptian to the time of Cleopatra, he would have felt quite at home.

Now fast-forward another 1,000 years from 30 BCE to the Middle Ages. You'd find there had been some advances, but the world of work—farming, livestock, hand-crafted goods, trading over water by sailing ship—was pretty much the same as it had always been. Human life expectancy was the same too, and most people died of infectious diseases, just as they always had.

After the Black Death ravaged Europe in the 1350s—wiping out a third of the population—the technological acceleration began. Within three centuries we saw the Industrial Revolution emerge, followed by the Information Age. Technology progressed by leaps and bounds. Democracy emerged as a new political system. Nations began to be governed by the rule of law. We learned about the size and configuration of the Solar System and the galaxies.

Not only did technology advance, but the *rate* of advancement increased, like a jet picking up speed for takeoff. In 1965, Gordon Moore proposed what has become known as Moore's Law, which posited a doubling every year in the number of components per integrated circuit. Ten years later, looking forward to the next decade, he revised the forecast to a doubling every two years, a compound annual growth rate of 41 percent. Since then, his prediction has held.

The relationship between employer and employee has been changing at an accelerated pace as well. For tens of thousands of years, employers could own slaves and exert control over every aspect of their lives. That practice was abolished only a century and a half ago. Gone, too, are indentured servants. But for much of the Industrial Age, employers, resisted only by organized unions and government regulation, could dictate wages and working conditions. Many, like the Pullman Company in Chicago, set up systems whereby the employees were indebted to the company. George Pullman created Pullman Town, a village where he made all of his workers live in houses he rented to them. In 1894, when an economic depression hit, Pullman cut wages by 25 percent and refused to reduce rents, which caused the employees to be in debt to the company. One employee, a seamstress named Jennie Curtis, testified before Congress, "My father worked for the Pullman company for thirteen years. He died last September, and I paid the rent to the Pullman company up to the time he died; I was boarding at the time of my father's death. He being laid off and sick for three months, owed the Pullman company $60 at the time of his death for back rent, and the company made me, out of my small earnings, pay that rent due from my father."[1]

While we no longer have "company towns" in America, the fact remains that too many employers have traditionally viewed labor as a commodity to be purchased at the lowest possible price. Over and over again, we see this as a mistake. Just one example was the infamous case of Circuit City, which at its peak in the year 2000 employed more than 60,000 people at 616 locations across the United States. But in 2003 the company abruptly converted its highly regarded commissioned salespeople into hourly "product specialists," while laying off 3,900 others. The move saved the company about $130 million per year in labor costs. But guess what? The change *cost* the company in lost sales far more than it saved and set it on the road to decline. In 2007, the starting wage for new employees was dropped from $8.75 an hour down to $7.40 an hour ($6.55 being the federal minimum wage at the time). It also laid off approximately 3,400 better-paid associates and hired replacements at a lower wage.

On November 10, 2008, Circuit City filed for bankruptcy protection under Chapter 11 of the U.S. Bankruptcy Code. Over 30,000 employees lost their jobs in the liquidation.

The first two decades of the twenty-first century saw employers try to cut labor costs by using an increasing number of freelance workers who were responsible for their own taxes, retirement plans, and healthcare. The global financial crisis in 2007 and 2008 accelerated this trend, and by 2017, an estimated 55 million Americans were part of the gig economy, or 36 percent of the workforce. A CNBC report in February 2020—just before the Covid-19 pandemic hit—stated that the number of gig workers had surged by 15 percent since 2010. That was about six million more workers involved in the gig economy than a decade earlier.[2]

In 2020–2021, the Covid-19 pandemic massively disrupted the world of work. Businesses across the globe closed their offices and, thanks to the internet, millions of workers began working remotely, from home. They joined the millions who had already bailed out of the traditional employer-employee relationship to become freelance gig workers.

Looking ahead, we see no slowing of the pace of workplace disruption. In fact, as the United States slowly recovered from Covid-19 in late 2021, a new problem emerged: employees began quitting in droves.

The Great Resignation

The wave of employee walkouts was given a name—"the Great Resignation." In August 2021, 4.3 million workers left their jobs. The "quits" rate (as it's called by statisticians) rose to 2.9 percent, an increase of 242,000 from the previous month, which saw a rate of 2.7 percent, according to the US Department of Labor's Job Openings and Labor Turnover Survey. Bar and restaurant employees as well as retail staff quit in numbers not seen since December 2000.[3]

Historically, quits have been seen as a measure of the level of confidence of workers who feel they are secure in finding employment elsewhere. Workers reportedly left their jobs because of health concerns and childcare issues unique to the circumstances of the Covid-19 pandemic— or more broadly, what we call the Covid-19 economy.

The BBC put it bluntly: "Foremost, workers are taking decisions to leave based on how their employers treated them—or didn't treat them— during the pandemic. Ultimately, workers stayed at companies that offered support, and darted from those that didn't."[4]

As far as millions of employees are concerned, in the Covid-19 economy, happy workplaces are the new mandate. An organization's growth and prosperity will be based on its ability to institutionalize and scale happiness as an integral part of their enterprise strategy.

Unfortunately, many leaders are blind to this reality, and they cling to the old belief that simply paying employees more money or giving them an employee lounge with free bagels on Friday is the answer. While compensation matters, and free bagels are better than no bagels, being happy at work goes much deeper. It's about the everyday experience of working, the mission of the organization, the opportunities for both professional advancement and lifelong learning, the place of the organization in the community, and the long-term relationships that a happy workplace can foster.

Why Employee Happiness Matters

It may seem crazy that we have to have a section with this title, but given how many companies like Amazon promote the misery of entry-level employees as a business strategy, we need to offer evidence that employee happiness (which for various reasons Amazon will eventually be forced to embrace, just as Walmart has) is a good thing that contributes to long-term profits and growth.

Again, we recognize that happiness is subjective, and that in addition to simply asking employees if they're happy (which we'll do in the pages ahead), it's useful to detect the level of employee happiness by its effects. Let's go back to the ancient Egyptians who built the Great Pyramid of Giza. We know some external facts about their lives. They ate a very good, high-protein diet. They were housed comfortably. If they died on the job (and with 10,000 working at a time, deaths were bound to occur), they were buried with honor next to the pyramid itself. They gave their work gangs names. They kept coming to the site for 30 years (no doubt many fathers and then sons). These conditions sound pretty good for 5,000 years ago!

But were the workers individually and collectively *happy?*

We cannot ask them, so we may never know for certain. But we do know from modern jobs that happiness is not related to the degree of difficulty or danger on a job. Plenty of soldiers, sailors, cops, firemen, and coal miners are happy people who live long lives.

We see happiness as reflected in such metrics as employee engagement, absenteeism, productivity, and innovation. These are the fruits of happiness, however you define it.

In "The Impact of Employee Engagement on Performance," *Harvard Business Review* found that 71 percent of surveyed executives ranked employee engagement as very important to achieving overall organizational success. Mike Rickheim, vice president of talent management at Newell Rubbermaid, a global consumer goods company, said that engagement "is not just a warm, fuzzy thing. It's about giving people the tools they need to succeed in their careers, which in turn drives the outcomes that we're seeking in the marketplace. When you look at it through that lens, when people have the tools they need to succeed, feel good about their personal growth opportunities, and receive the appropriate rewards and recognition for their contributions, it's a win-win proposition."[5]

A study by Franklin Health Research found that a two-year program instituted by an employer found that employee well-being started low and increased to exceed community worker averages, approaching significance. Increases in employer support for well-being were associated with improved well-being and productivity, and well-being improvement was associated with higher productivity across all measures.[6]

In the United Kingdom, the iOpener Institute found that in a study with 41,000 respondents, the happiest employees took one-tenth the amount of sick leave of their least happy colleagues, were six times more energized, intended to stay twice as long in their organizations, and were twice as productive. They also looked at unhappy employees and found they spend only 40 percent of their time on task. In a five-day workweek, that's *just two days a week*. This lack of productivity represents a huge cost to any organization.[7]

Researchers at the University of Warwick found that happy employees work harder. In the laboratory, they found happiness made people around 12 percent more productive. Dr. Eugenio Proto said, "We have shown that happier subjects are more productive. The same pattern appears in four different experiments. This research will provide some guidance for management in all kinds of organizations, that they should strive to make their workplaces emotionally healthy for their workforce."[8]

The list of similar studies goes on and on. And by the way, if you're looking for research studies that suggest *unhappy* workers are more productive, you should keep searching. There aren't any.

The Two Great Challenges

It's fair to say that in the next decade, organizations large and small will be facing two great challenges.

The first challenge is that we live in a time of hypercompetition. This level of competition requires that we operate lean organizations with a maximal return on assets and human capital. This cannot be done without great people doing great work. You cannot compete using employees who are "just putting in their time" and working from paycheck to paycheck. Increasingly, *your competitor* is trying to lure away your best employees and candidates by offering a happy workplace.

The second challenge is the fact that there has been a multigenerational shift in the way in which we look at work. In the old days we were taught to exchange our time for a paycheck; in other words, "our lives for cash." The emphasis was on salary and benefits. You took your hard-earned money home and bought the stuff that made you happy.

Today, employees across the generational spectrum are looking for work that is meaningful and provides personal growth and advancement opportunities while serving others. You can only get that in a happy workplace.

They're also focused on the promise of inclusion and diversity, and to achieve that we have to begin with a culture of happiness that loves and respects all employees and stakeholders equally. Correspondingly, we need to implement rapid organizational cultural transformation to meet the demands of a highly competitive marketplace and workforce.

The question is, how can an organization measure happiness, get leadership buy-in, design a happiness framework, put it into place across the entire organization from top to bottom, measure again, and keep adapting to meet changing conditions?

The Happy Work Principle

How can an employer determine if his or her employees are happy, and then take action to increase their happiness (and therefore their productivity)?

The Happy Work Principle is the answer. It provides organizations the framework that creates a culture that embodies their organizational mission and provides employees and owners alike the opportunity for personal and professional growth while serving others.

In the following chapters, we'll explore how your organization can complete its transformation into a happy workplace—*and more profitable workplace*—by taking it one step at a time.

The journey can only begin if the critical first step is taken, which is leadership acceptance and prioritization. Leaders must embrace a set of realities that, when considered together, drive toward the inescapable conclusion that the organization will benefit, thrive, and prosper when all of its stakeholders are happy with their work.

Here are the realities that need to be recognized and endorsed:

- Leaders must be dedicated to creating a culture that supports diversity and equity. Fairness goes beyond diverse workgroups; everyone should enjoy the benefits of equity and fairness.
- It's a reality that over 90 percent of potential employees will do a background check on your organization using websites such as Glassdoor and others. Organizations with bad Glassdoor ratings will fail to attract the best talent. These assets will instead go to work for your competitor.
- Happy employees reduce absenteeism due to sickness and thereby lower overall health care costs. They reduce the risk of workmen's compensation claims, unemployment costs, and employees filing lawsuits against the employer
- Happy employees achieve greater productivity and exhibit less presenteeism—defined as lost productivity when employees are not fully functioning in the workplace because of an illness, injury, or other condition. In other words, they show up for work, but don't accomplish much.

- Lower employee turnover and higher retention reduce the cost of hiring and training replacement employees. The Society for Human Resource Management (SHRM) has reported that on average it costs a company 6 to 9 months of an employee's salary to replace him or her. For an employee making $60,000 per year, that comes out to $30,000 to $45,000 in recruiting and training costs.[9]
- Happy employees are future-oriented and drive growth. They embrace innovation and are more likely to adapt to disruption.
- Today's customers demand and expect superior customer experiences at every touchpoint, and the only way to deliver better experiences is through happy employees.
- A happy culture is not just about younger employees; the desire for a happy work structure is alive and well across all generations.
- Investors are increasingly interested in putting their money into socially responsible companies with a track record of happy employees. They're also increasingly reluctant to support recalcitrant companies that are stuck in the twentieth century.
- Results obtained by hard-nosed Wall Street investors whose number one priority is their return on investment demonstrate that a happy workplace is often more profitable than an indifferent or fear-based workplace. If you want to make a lot of money for a long period of time, your best bet is to make the Happy Work Principle an integral part of your everyday operations.

The Three Facets of Workplace Happiness

This book will reveal how the importance of the happiness of a worker—whether a janitor or CEO—can be seen like a three-sided coin.

First, when the worker interacts with a customer, it stands to reason the customer wants to engage with a happy representative rather than one who's unhappy, surly, rude, or indifferent. This has economic consequences.

A customer who must deal with an unhappy employee is likely to spend less, post a negative comment on social media, or even take their business elsewhere. Conversely, a customer who deals with a happy employee is likely to spend more, recommend the business to their friends and family, and remain a loyal customer.

Second, when the worker interacts with other employees—peers, subordinates, or superiors—then it also stands to reason that happiness in the form of cooperation, empathy, and optimism should be valued as well. Negative energy is draining and distracting, while positive energy is energizing and uplifting.

The third context is the employee's attitude toward the job itself. An unhappy worker will be absent more often, will minimize contact with other employees, and will have no enthusiasm for innovation. He or she will try to work the least amount for the same paycheck, cover up mistakes, and shift blame for setbacks onto other people. The happy employee will enjoy coming to work, be a good team player, and seek out challenges. He or she will accept responsibility for mistakes and help others who may be lagging behind.

Take Action!

- ✓ The Happy Work Principle provides organizations the framework for a culture that embodies their organizational mission and provides employees and owners alike the opportunity for personal and professional growth while serving others.
- ✓ Many research studies have found that happy workers are more productive and therefore more profitable for the organization. As far as we know, no study has shown that *unhappy* workers are more productive.
- ✓ Employers are facing two great challenges. The first challenge is that we live in a time of hypercompetition, which raises the stakes and challenges all of us to

excel. The second challenge is that there has been a multigenerational shift in the way in which we look at work, and workers young and old alike are looking for a vocation that is meaningful and provides personal growth and advancement opportunities while serving others.

✓ The journey to workplace happiness can begin only if the critical first step is taken by leadership, which is acceptance and prioritization.

✓ There are three facets to employee happiness:

1. When the worker interacts with a customer, happy interactions increase the odds of a bigger sale.

2. When the worker interacts with other employees, then happiness in the form of cooperation, empathy, and optimism is energizing and uplifting.

3. The employee's attitude toward the job itself. A happy employee will enjoy coming to work, be a good team player, and seek out challenges, and therefore be more productive.

CHAPTER 3

Measuring Happiness and Its Benefits

In business, it's become axiomatic that if you want to manage a process or outcome, you need to measure it, and not just once but repeatedly over time. You look at the results of your measurements to determine the effectiveness of your effort.

If you want to manage industrial production, you have to measure it—not once, but on a regular basis. How many units per day are you making? Can you increase the rate so that when you measure it tomorrow, you'll see faster production?

If you want to manage your company's social media presence, you must measure it and then take steps to change the results of your measurement. For example, you need to reduce the percentage of negative comments and increase the number of positive ones.

If you want to increase the level of happiness in your organization, then you have to begin by measuring it. Having a baseline, you then take action and measure it again at some future date.

The challenge is that happiness is a human emotion. You can *ask* people if they're happy, but you might not get a straight answer. Humans are funny that way. We sometimes have difficulty articulating our feelings. What's more, many people will tell you what they think you want to hear. We all know "tough guys" (and gals) who, if they were to fall down and break their leg, would get up and proclaim, "I'm good! No problem! Let's keep going!" We also know the "sad sack" or "Debbie downer" types who should be perfectly happy, but if you ask them how they feel, they say, "I'm terrible. Nothing is going right. I'm going lie down and cry."

Since people can be unreliable when you ask them how they feel, then perhaps the next best way to measure happiness is to note their *behavior*. As Sgt. Maj. Mark Thompson said, soldiers talk with their feet. So do employees. Therefore, the simple measurement of employee retention would seem to be a good litmus test. Payscale publishes a useful list of companies with the highest employee turnover, which might correlate to employee happiness. At the top of the list are Massachusetts Mutual Life Insurance (average tenure just 0.8 years!), Amazon.com (1 year), AFLAC (1 year), and Google (1.1 years).[1]

Companies with the lowest employee churn rate—and presumably the most happy employees—tend to include manufacturing companies with skilled employees who make things. The list features names including Eastman Kodak (20 years), Aleris Rolled Products (16.5), United Airlines (12.6), Visteon Corporation (11.3), and General Motors (10.3).[2]

The current CEO and president of GM, Mary Barra, first went to work there at the age of 18, as a co-op student assigned to inspect hoods and door panels. Clearly, by any yardstick she was happy to work at GM, because 34 years later she was named chief executive officer. She has never taken a paycheck from any other company.

You can surmise that aside from company culture, the *type* of job has a lot to do with employee retention and—most likely—employee happiness. Many jobs are entry level, like burger flippers or telemarketers. You expect young people to populate those jobs, get some training and work experience, and then move upward to another job that requires more skill and pays better. In fact, it might be unusual to see someone work the counter at McDonald's or be a stockperson at Walmart for more than a year or two. Pretty quickly the pleasure at having a paying job—*any* job—will wear off and dissatisfaction will rear its head.

Many successful people have fond memories of their first transitory entry-level job. Jay Leno, who worked at McDonald's in high school, speaks highly of the experience. Once the store manager told him to destroy a load of potatoes that may have been contaminated. "That was very impressive to me," Leno remembered. "The standards for quality were quite high. It was one of those life lessons I never forgot."[3]

You never know what will give people pleasure. There are some people who take a low-skills job and they stick with it year after year because they like it. Consider the story of Faye Mudd. On January 1, 1981, shortly after her graduation from Waterloo High School in St. Louis, she was hired by the Waterloo School District as a custodian. Over the years, she worked as a janitor, crossing guard, and ticket taker at football games. She did this for 40 years before retiring on January 29, 2021. "I've worked for the school ever since I was little bitty," she told the *Republic Times*. "In grade school, there were days when we got to take turns working in the cafeteria. Then, I worked in the cafeteria all through high school." What made her happy? She said her favorite part of working in the school district was the people, including students and coworkers. "The students made my day. It was like family."[4]

Of course, once upon a time you could support a family by working full-time at a single low-paying job. Those days are over—which would be the subject of another book!

The Misery Reward

Any discussion of employee happiness must also touch upon a peculiar and yet pernicious syndrome that affects many workplaces in the industrialized world, particularly in the United States and Japan.

It's what I call the Misery Reward.

Basically, it goes like this. Many managers want to be certain they're squeezing every last drop of productivity from their employees who, after all, are an expense. As part of their measurement of employee dedication to their jobs, they look at the emotional state of the employee. The idea is that an employee who's working to his or her limit will be tired, a bit disoriented, and definitely not "happy." In contrast, an employee who's cheerful and seems to have boundless energy is obviously not working hard or long enough.

For example, consider two administrators, Lisa and Susan. Their boss is Charlie.

Whenever Charlie enters Lisa's office, he sees her desk piled high with papers, folders, and files. She's hunched over her computer, frowning. When he asks her to complete a task by end of day, she sighs and says, "Yes, okay—but I'm so hopelessly swamped with work I cannot possibly do it before tomorrow." She radiates the vibe that if you put one more straw on her aching back, she'd break.

When Charlie enters Susan's office, he sees a clean desk. Susan works at her computer with a smile on her face. When he asks her to do a task, she says, "You need this by five o'clock? It's a priority? No problem. You'll have it." She radiates the vibe that whatever you throw at her, she'll handle with aplomb.

According to the law of the Misery Reward, Charlie—who's not a very bright manager—will conclude that Lisa is the more valuable, hardworking employee. He'll think so purely on the basis of her dramatic display of misery. Susan, he may conclude, is just coasting and maybe even expendable. If layoffs must be considered, Susan may very well find herself at the top of the list, even if she's objectively more productive than Lisa.

Certainly, in some workplaces it can be dangerous to appear too happy. This plays into the well-known fact that in the pre-Covid era, American workers were often afraid to take vacation time that was owed to them. A Glassdoor survey found that 23 percent of employee respondents didn't take all of their earned vacation time. And 66 percent of those who took time off said they didn't cut ties completely—they worked remotely during their time away from the office.[5] And when offered unlimited paid time off, employees actually take less time off on average, even though under typical "PTO" policies they don't have the traditional option of cashing out unused vacation time at the end of the year. In other words, employers play a cruel game. They say, "Sure, go ahead, take all the vacation time you want!" To many employees, this is like the spider talking to the fly. They're afraid that if they take even a reasonable vacation, they'll be seen as being a slacker.

Why do so many employees give away time and money to their employers? For many, the answer is fear. It's loss of promotion opportunities, loss of bonuses, even loss of job when layoffs are on the table.

Many cynical employers want their employees to be "happy-scared"— that is, happy enough to not quit, and yet sufficiently scared to work harder to stay in favor with the boss. It's a dicey approach. Obviously, at a place like an Amazon fulfillment center, you might say that Amazon wants its employees to be 5 percent happy and 95 percent terrified. Well, it works, which means that Amazon chews up and spits out employees the way the TV show *Survivor* cycles through contestants.

Why Traditional Employee Surveys Don't Work

In the old days, employers didn't care if their employees were "happy" or "engaged," or had "good morale," or whatever the word was. If you showed up on time, did your job, and weren't drunk or a troublemaker, that was enough. You took your paycheck and went home, where you could be happy to your heart's content. In fact, it was assumed—especially for farm-work and manufacturing jobs, of which the United States had more than any other nation—that you would *not* be happy at work. Work was tough, and the purpose of work was to earn money so that you could *become* happy by buying the stuff you wanted—a car, a refrigerator, a TV set.

If your job was customer-facing, such as sales or customer service, then you were expected to *act* happy. Whether you really were happy was irrelevant.

Over time, as the farm sector shrank and manufacturing jobs gave way to service jobs, workers began to think about their overall quality of life. They began to think that maybe they should be happy at work. After all, many people spent as much time on the job as at home, especially after you added in commuting time, which got longer and longer). In the early twentieth century, most factory workers *walked* to work.) Employers began to think about employee morale, because even the most Scrooge-like employers realized that disgruntled or unhappy employees were less productive, absent more often, and even liable to commit transgressions like pilfering and sabotage. The goal was to ensure your employees were "engaged," which meant "focused on the job." Whether they were happy was not the issue.

Employers began taking employee engagement surveys. Many workers quickly perceived the annual ritual to be meaningless and irrelevant. Opinions were collected from employees, but they rarely saw any significant change as a result. Year after year, virtually the same questions were asked, and the outcome was sadly predictable: All talk, no action. That's how the cycle went each year.

The outcome?

Even today, the traditional employee engagement survey process can actually *aggravate* and *provoke* increased employee disengagement! It's more honest to say to someone, "I don't care about you," than to lie and say, "I care about you," and then turn your back on them.

Aside from employer inaction, here are some of the reasons why traditional employee engagement surveys fail.

- **They ask irrelevant questions.** Surveys often ask generic questions about the company's operational structure rather than asking questions about happiness. For instance, they'd ask employees questions about pay, benefits, and promotions rather than asking questions about their feelings. Questions should focus on employees' perceptions, not organization benefits.

    Questions are frequently too vague, making it difficult for companies to get accurate information from employees. For example, take this common employee engagement question: "Does your manager value your talents and the contributions you make?" This is highly subjective and difficult to answer because (for instance) a manager may *generally* value the employee's talents and contributions, but on *one occasion* slighted the employee, which then gave the employee a grudge to nurse.

- **They imply retribution.** Employees need to have a high level of trust in their leaders before they answer any survey honestly. If management really wants to find out who said what on a typical survey, they can easily do so. Leaders who receive unpleasant feedback often concentrate on it and begin hunting to find out the source of the discontent. Consequently, even when surveys are supposedly confidential, employees can distrust the system and give inaccurate answers.

- **They ask employees questions only during the survey period.** When survey time draws near, leaders exhibit enthusiasm and broadcast the fact they want to "listen." But annual or infrequent surveys are like annual employee reviews— sharp feelings from the recent past are likely to be subsumed into a general lassitude. Responses tend to have recency bias, where employees focus on what's happened in the immediate past, even just the past few days, instead of having a more holistic perspective.

- **Employees say contradictory things.** Remember, every employee has a baseline level of anxiety about his or her position with the organization. They know they can be laid off at any time, even from the nicest company. When they fill out ordinary surveys, this stress cannot be ignored. For example, *Inc.* magazine noted this not uncommon dilemma. Human resources software company Ultimate Software did a series of employee surveys. "Through our surveys," said chief people officer, Vivian Maza, "we had increasingly heard from employees wishing for more time off throughout the year. At the same time, we had managers coming to us saying that some of their direct reports weren't taking the time off when they probably should." The employees asked for more time off because, well, that's what employees do—and yet they were afraid that if they actually used their time off, company leaders would think they were slacking.[6]

Here are some types of employee survey formats that are popular—but come up short.

- **Net promoter score.** The net promoter score asks employees one simple question: "Would you recommend the workplace to someone you know?" "No" is bad, "yes" is good. The problem with any such one-question survey is that it provides leaders with zero actionable insight. If the employee replies "no," then what do you do? What makes the employee unhappy? Is it his boss? Lousy food in the break room? Harassment? A long commute? No interest in the product? Without a clue as to why the employee is unhappy, the information is useless.
- **The Goldilocks question.** Here's another one-question survey. You ask the employee if their workload is "too much, too little, or just right." Let's get real: How many employees will answer "too little"? A good guess would be zero. On the other end, how many will admit to "too much"? Probably zero. Most will say, "about right," which provides you with no useful information.

  The Goldilocks question can be applied to any scenario, like if they feel like they're getting enough autonomy, or if they're getting enough one-on-one time with their manager. How many employees will answer honestly? Very few.
- **Multiple choice.** When an organization depends upon multiple choice questions, it puts a boundary around employees' honesty. Instead of sharing their opinions and voice, they're

compelled to choose between answers put before them by their leaders.

The Survey Industrial Complex

The proclamation that surveys are a "scam" may seem a bit shocking, but in most cases, it's simply true. We have created a "survey industrial complex" of organizations that have built the perfect business model. These busy industrialists develop a survey algorithm, charge an organization to have their employees complete the survey, and then report out to the client in a dashboard their employees' level of job satisfaction. Although this approach is a lucrative business model, it's also an incredible disservice to the organizations that spend tens of millions of dollars attempting to glean insights through this outdated and fractional model. The survey industry is massive, and it's also incredibly profitable: GlobeNewsWire projects the global online survey software market to grow at a compound annual growth rate (CAGR) of 13.04 percent from $4.870 billion in 2019 to $10.162 billion in 2025.[7]

Knowledge Sourcing Intelligence estimates the global online survey software market will grow even faster, at a CAGR of 16.04 percent to reach a market size of $13.796 billion in 2026. Big players in the online survey industry include Zoho Corporation Pvt. Ltd., Medallia, Confirmit AS, Inqwise, SurveyMonkey, Campaign Monitor, QuestionPro Survey Software, and Qualtrics. You cannot ignore the power of data monetization, the process of collecting data from the target audience to develop greater insights into the market and generate revenue with this data. The data monetization industry uses many tools including online survey software to collect the data for monetization. This market is anticipated to grow at a CAGR of 6.02 percent (source: KSI) and will create a significant opportunity for the online survey software market.[8]

This massive industry is essentially an online vending machine that delivers minimal value at an extremely high cost. The companies that produce surveys love this model because it's profitable, and truthfully most organizational leaders like it because it's the easiest and fastest way to check the box on employee insights while creating authoritative-looking graphs and charts.

Knowing Where to Tap

The benefit of a survey is to glean insights as to where to direct detailed inquiry.

You may have heard this story. A woman's car rolls to a stop in front of a mechanic's shop. She tells the mechanic her engine suddenly quit. The mechanic lifts the hood of the car. He then pulls out a hammer and taps on a particular part of the engine. He then asks the woman to go ahead and start the car. Instantly, the car roars to life. The woman asks the repairman how much for the repair, and he replies, twenty dollars and ten cents. She asks why the unusual price? He replies that it's ten cents for the tapping and twenty dollars for knowing where to tap.

The benefit of a survey is to learn where to tap to create innovations and improvements. If a survey doesn't deliver those insights, it's nothing but worthless data. In our practice, we use a system that focuses on what each employee loves and hates about their job to determine their net level of satisfaction. We refer to our approach as the Net Employee Experience (NEX). We believe this approach is superior to traditional methods, but we also realize that it would be disingenuous—in other words a scam!—to suggest that a survey alone would give our client the information that they need to be able to drive a cultural transformation of happiness.

The Holistic Approach
Toward Real Employee Insights

Surveys can be very useful in identifying areas that need additional investigation.

For example, when you go to your doctor for an annual physical, they will run a complete blood panel. Once the blood panel returns, the doctor will look to the right side of the blood panel to identify areas that are outside of the normal range. For example, if your total blood count turned out to be low, it would tell your doctor that they need to identify the reasons why your blood count was low.

The blood panel is not a *diagnosis* but a *screening tool* that suggests areas of inquiry. If the results raise a "red flag," then the real work of the doctor would begin. He or she would then have to determine the reason for the low count. Perhaps your iron level was too low, or there was some potential internal bleeding. Again, the blood panel was just used to find out if anything was out of range so the doctor could begin deeper inquiry to potential problem areas.

The same facts are in play when it comes to running an employee engagement or satisfaction survey. Based on the survey alone, you will not have a diagnosable understanding of your employee's current sentiments. You'll need to drill deeper into areas that you identified as being problematic in your survey.

Most surveys look at the wrong things. They try to determine an employee's willingness to promote you or an employee's level of engagement. These factors in many ways are irrelevant. What we really need to understand across the various anatomical features of employee happiness is where your employee stands from the perspective of the love/hate sentiment.

So how do we get comprehensive insights about your employee's state of happiness that also help us target areas for further inquiry? It turns out there are *three* dimensions to gaining the insight we need, yet most companies stop at one—the survey. Following my doctor analogy, they get a blood test and simply report what items are out of range. Then they simply move on without deeper inquiry and without a treatment plan.

The Three Dimensions of Employee Insights

The best organizations in the world leverage a holistic approach toward gaining insights about their employees' current state of happiness. This approach provides far more accurate data and important insights that go far beyond the screening-tool survey approach. The benefits of a holistic approach include significantly improved insights and actionable discoveries that result in rapid improvement in overall quality of work life.

1. Pre-Survey "State of Play" Analysis

Continuing with my medical analogy, a good doctor won't begin requesting tests until he or she has completed a thorough consultation. The consultation will look at known factors. For example, if the patient is overweight, this will impact the types of tests that the doctor needs to conduct to make certain that they screen for known disease processes in overweight patients. This would include cardiovascular conditions, diabetes, and hyperlipidemia, just to name a few. The consultation may further discover that the patient has orthopedic problems as a result of their weight, which may require a specialist such as an orthopedic surgeon to inquire about the physical limitation challenges. The consultation may discover that the patient is suffering from depression or stress. Correspondingly, the doctor would want to know more about that in order to offer mental health resources.

In other words, the doctor would never just say, "Thanks for coming in, let me run the standard blood test and I'll get back to you with the results soon." Yet that's exactly what we do with traditional surveys. We are indiscriminate about the way in which we dispatch meaningless and generic surveys.

The best organizations frontload the process with a comprehensive *state of play analysis* that looks at the unique and special challenges and opportunities of each organization. This allows them to architect a state of play analysis to get to the insights that will move them toward optimal health.

A key question that must be asked is whether the organization is ready for change. It's like when you construct a skyscraper, the first thing you need to do is perform a complete analysis of the subsoil and bedrock to determine its suitability for a new building. If it's suitable, then you proceed. But for various reasons it may not be suitable, in which case you must do remediation until it's ready. Likewise, if the people in your organization are resistant to new ideas—even ones that will measurably help them and make them happier—then your first task must be to change the culture and perhaps even provide training, so that you can then present them with new information they'll embrace.

2. Survey Design, Evaluation, and Reporting

I'm surprised that the overwhelming majority of employee surveys look very much the same as they did in the 1950s. They ask obvious questions that employees typically answer dishonestly or inaccurately. But don't blame the employees; they've been put into an unfortunate predicament. The surveys ask them to answer questions about the organization that provides their paycheck, and they're not particularly likely to say anything derogatory even in so-called anonymous surveys. Most employees suspect that if a survey is dispatched digitally, it can easily be traced back to them, and any adverse comments could be detrimental to their career pathway.

Many organizations architect surveys that don't take into consideration a thoughtful analysis of the organization and its current state of readiness as it relates to cultural transformation toward happiness.

The right way to do this is simple: Design a survey that embraces a comprehensive and thoughtful assessment of the organization's challenges, problems, opportunities, and needs. Then you evaluate the survey based on the overarching assessment of the organization, which allows you to create specific recommendations to target areas for additional inquiry. This is how you get the best insights and create an amazing results-focused happiness strategy.

3. Collaborative Ideation

I've had the great honor of facilitating collaborative ideation sessions and what we call *happiness hackathons*. These programs are incredibly effective at soliciting authentic and hard-hitting insights from employees. Employees are emboldened by other employees to answer questions more bravely about what's not working and what really needs to happen in order to build a culture of happiness. We also leverage individuals in group interviews in order to get useful insights from employees that we aggregate along with our survey data to build out specific recommendations on what needs to be done quickly to move the happiness needle within an organization.

Take Action!

- ✓ In business, if you want to manage a process or outcome, you need to measure it over time. If you want to increase the level of happiness in your organization, then you have to begin by measuring it. Having a baseline, you then take positive action to influence it, and measure it again at some future date.
- ✓ Different things and situations make different people happy. Some people hold a low-skills job and they stay with it year after year because they like it. Others need leadership and responsibility to be happy. You have to recognize and leverage these differences.
- ✓ Sadly, some managers view employee misery as an asset and proof they're squeezing every last drop of productivity from their employees. If this is your mindset, do yourself a favor and change it. Your investors will thank you.
- ✓ By asking the wrong questions in the wrong way, traditional employee engagement survey process can actually *aggravate* and *provoke* increased employee disengagement.
- ✓ Most surveys do not provide a *diagnosis* but serve as a *screening tool* to suggest areas of inquiry. They can tell you that an employee is unhappy, but they don't

tell you *why*. The Net Employee Experience (NEX) system focuses on what each employee loves and hates about their job in order to determine their net level of satisfaction.

CHAPTER 4

The RealRatings Happiness Solution

Despite the challenge of measuring something as subjective as happiness, we must forge ahead without flinching. This is because we need to do it to provide guidance, and because there is a way of measuring happiness by how much it changes. In other words, once we have established a baseline level of what our employees call happiness, we can apply the Happy Work Principle across the organization, let it percolate for a year, and then survey our employees again. We can see if, when using the same yardstick, there has been any improvement. If the answer is "yes," then we maintain the effort. If the answer is "no," then we know that we need to try a different approach.

In my previous book, *What Customers Hate*, I introduced a revolutionary new form of customer survey called RealRatings. The system is based on a simple fact: What customers choose to buy is based not only on what they *love the most* but what they *hate the least*. This seems so obvious as to be almost silly, but it's even more amazing to think that traditional surveys don't measure this.

Think about it. When you choose a bank—say for your mortgage—do you choose the bank you love the most? Of course not. No one loves the bank they get their mortgage from. You choose the bank you hate the least—the one that offers the most tolerable deal and service.

When you're on the highway and you're really hungry and you've got to eat, and the only choices are fast-food restaurants, you're going to choose the burger joint that you hate the least.

When you sign up for a cable TV provider—yup, you'll choose the one you hate the least.

And when you look for a job because you need to earn a living, do you always have the luxury of getting the job you love? For millions of people, the question is laughable. You don't get the dream job you love. You take the job you hate the least.

The RealRatings survey asks the respondent what he or she *loves* about something and also what they *hate* about it. That's right—we want to know what they dislike about our product or service or company. This is not so strange—after all, customers are venting exactly that on public websites like Yelp and Glassdoor. People are quite comfortable broadcasting to the world what they hate about stores, restaurants, schools—and their own workplaces.

Most survey systems are afraid to ask what I call the "hate questions," or they structure questions that have a neutral response. Why? Because the people who administer the surveys don't want to hear about what you hate. It seems too volatile and too provocative.

The RealRatings system creates a score of two sets of numbers: Hatepoints™ and Lovepoints™.

Hatepoints are measured across four negative experiences, from 1 (slight hate) to 4 (maximum hate).

Lovepoints are measured across four positive experiences, from 1 (slight love) to 4 (maximum love).

The RealRating is the total of hate points subtracted from the love points.

You will note that in both cases, there is no middle fifth choice of "undecided" or "not sure." I purposely designed this patent pending program to *not* be a five-point survey, as neutrality—in other words, having a point in the middle that is neutral—makes it easy for the employee to avoid answering the question by choosing the bland middle ground.

The RealRating represents the Net Employee Experience (or NEX) by subtracting the Hatepoints from the Lovepoints to produce a score. This score is very useful because it's expressly asking what the employee loves and hates about the organization. This provides actionable insights that an organization can use to rapidly fix the dislikes to significantly improve their RealRatings NEX score.

How does this matter in real life?

It matters because if you want to improve employee happiness—and therefore engagement, productivity, loyalty, innovation, and all the other things that happiness produces—then it's just as important to *remove those things your employees hate* as it is to *strengthen those things your employees love*. Both are equally important.

For example, you might think that free bagels in the break room is a benefit your employees will love, and therefore will make them happy. But what you may not realize is that what your employees *hate* is that the break room is located at the opposite end of the floor from the bathrooms, and if they want to go to the bathroom on their break, they don't have time to run to the other end of the building to the break room. They don't care about free bagels as much as they care about never being able to visit the break room in the first place.

In order to get to an actionable employee experience rating, you have to find out what the employees hate and subtract that from what they love.

RealRatings surveys are custom architected to address the uniqueness of the employee experience (EX) and to select the proper linguistics in order to glean accurate responses. This provides you with two very significant improvements in terms of employee experience insights. First, it provides far better insights as to what your employees do *not* like, so as to provide a net experience that is far more accurate, albeit perhaps less flattering. The second benefit is that these insights will allow you to extinguish hate points through new innovations while optimizing the love points.

The Three Dimensions of Employee Happiness

Businesses deploy employee surveys to gain insights, but not many use them to produce better experiences. The problem of ignoring employee feedback is epidemic, and among many CEOs there's a general assumption that they're doing good customer experience work by simply churning surveys. Most of them are structured to make the organization feel that their employees are happy and everything is fine. It's like when your partner comes to you and says, "I just bought these new shoes for two hundred dollars. Aren't they wonderful? What do you think?"

What are you going to say, other than, "Yes, they are amazing shoes!"

In my experience, many organizations have a sense of how badly they cultivate employee happiness, but they don't want to memorialize the problem through a properly structured satisfaction rating program. The truth can be painful and require that you respond! But if you really want to reduce the hate points and boost the love points, you first need to look at the three dimensions of employee happiness.

Dimension 1: The Eight Employee Archetypes

Ever since the days of ancient Rome when personality types were first described by natural philosophers, we've known that people exhibit various patterns of behavior. These patterns can be grouped into types or archetypes. Just as you don't serve one type of customer (as my book *What Customers Hate* reveals), you don't employ one type of person.

The key thing to understand and appreciate is that human archetypes, including those of your employees, do not follow any rules of age, gender, or level of education. Contrary to the endless psycho-babbling about "Gen X" versus "Boomers" versus "Millennials," you cannot generalize behavior on these superficial attributes. You employ a range of archetypes who can be distinguished not by age or race or how they dress, but by their individual loves and hates. Across the range of employee archetypes, there's a well-established set of hate points and love points. In order to understand how to cultivate employee happiness, you need to know what they hate and love across eight general archetypes. I'll discuss this important point in much greater detail in the pages ahead.

Dimension 2: The Employee Touchpoint Journey

Every employee enters and serves across five well-defined touchpoints, and you must glean insights about their complete journey in order to determine where hate points and love points occur. Most organizations survey their employees with no regard to where they are in their journey.

Dimension 3: The Net Employee Experience

Most employee rating systems are reluctant to ask the hate questions, or they structure questions that elicit a neutral response. In order to get to an actionable employee experience rating—the RealRatings system—you have to find out what your employee hates and subtract that from what they love.

RealRatings surveys are carefully designed to address the uniqueness of the employee's experience and to select the proper linguistics in order to glean accurate responses. This provides you with two very significant improvements in measuring employee happiness. First, it provides far better insights as to what the employee does *not* like, so as to provide a net experience that is far more accurate, although perhaps more challenging for you, the leader. The second benefit is that these insights will allow you to minimize hate points while optimizing the love points.

The sum total of the employee's experience over the five touchpoints—which may extend in time to cover many years—is the NCX, or RealRating.

This is the measurement of what the employee hates and loves across the five touchpoints and a range of hate/love personas.

Personification Pigeonholing

Before we get into the nitty-gritty of surveying your employees, let's talk about the first challenge you face: If you have more than a handful of employees, your company comprises people with various personalities, viewpoints, and expectations. You might say your organization has psychological diversity. Operationally, this is a good thing! As you chart your way to growth and success, you need a variety of opinions. One person will see a problem or opportunity that someone else might miss. You don't want a company of robots who all think alike. That's a recipe for disaster.

The problem is that given this reality, figuring out who's happy and who's disgruntled takes skill and patience. People are individuals and they express themselves in their own ways. What pleases one person may displease another. A valued goal for one may seem pointless to another.

In an attempt to simplify the challenge, traditional organizations spend tens of millions of dollars each year attempting to pigeonhole their employees into groups of manageable archetypes. Typically, this is done for the benefit of the bureaucracy and not for the benefit of the employees. In other words, the organization is looking for ways to achieve better returns on capital or to spread their message in a way to attract talent without really thinking about the true impact their organizational culture has on the quality of life for employees. Even organizations using personification with the intention of improving the quality of life for their employees typically do it wrong.

Here are two of the ways they make mistakes—and how to avoid them.

Generational Personification

Many organizations like to use generational archetypes as a way to identify the various personality characteristics and motivators of an employee. To that end, sociologists and employers like to label the various generational groups and paint them as being fundamentally different from each other. You know them:

- **Gen Z, iGen, or Centennials:** Born 1996–2015
- **Millennials or Gen Y:** Born 1977–1995
- **Generation X:** Born 1965–1976
- **Baby Boomers:** Born 1946–1964
- **Traditionalists or Silent Generation:** Born 1945 and before

I suppose it's true that there are some superficial differences in the preferences and habits of these groups. A Gen Z kid is more likely to be a fan of Machine Gun Kelly than is a Boomer. (If you don't know who Machine Gun Kelly is, you've proved my point.) Members of the Silent Generation are concerned about their retirement nest egg, while the Gen Y person may be thinking about how to finance their first house.

But we're talking about how people *behave on the job.* Is a given employee dedicated, lazy, hardworking, dishonest, eager to please, indifferent? Are they a good team player? Do they want to lead or follow? Are they ready to jump ship for more money at some other job? Do they embrace innovation?

In reality, while there are certainly certain psychodynamics that come into play as a result of different societal outlooks in various generations, in the workplace, generational personification is a *big mistake.*

I know many Baby Boomers, including myself, who have an outlook on the workplace that matches what Millennials are supposed to want, and I have a daughter who is a Millennial who sees the world as Baby Boomers are reputed to see it.

The closer you look at these simplistic age categories, the more you see how inaccurate they are. Age is just *one* demographic data point among hundreds that make up who we are and our expectations. It's crazy to think that your age alone is a predictor of your approach to your job.

We have to resist pigeonholing current and potential employees by their generation because it doesn't work, and at its core it's prejudicial. We have to begin with the assumption that everyone wants to be honored and respected at work and that everyone wants to have a mission they believe in and that authors their own personal intellectual and emotional evolution while in the process of serving others.

Gender Personification

For centuries, it's been an ironclad axiom that in group situations, men and women behave differently. Men are dominant, women are submissive. Men like to "go it alone," women are collaborative. Men are admired for being aggressive, while assertive women are accused of being bitchy.

These stereotypes persist, and there are still plenty of businesses run by men who think "the gals" in the office are mainly decorative and who'll quit as soon as they get married and have kids. According to the Global Gender Gap Report 2020, based on the current rate of progress it will take another 100 years to achieve gender equality.[1] This prediction has been widely used as a clarion call to spur governments, NGOs, associations, investors, and companies into action.

In the face of the Covid-19 pandemic and economic crisis, efforts will have to be doubled if we are to avoid losing another 10 years to achieve gender equality. As the *New York Times* noted, around the world, in the Covid-19 economy, working women face difficult choices about whether to stay home if they haven't already been laid off. The effect may be particularly severe in countries like the United States, where the pandemic compounded inequalities that women already faced as a result of the lack of guaranteed paid maternity leave and affordable childcare.[2]

What does this have to do with personification pigeonholing? Gender bias can make leaders have assumptions about their employees based purely on gender. It can make a CEO assume incorrectly that a male vice president would be more dedicated to the company's success than a female vice president. It can make the CEO assume incorrectly that a particular female candidate would make different decisions than her male counterpart, or that she would have difficulty exerting leadership over her male subordinates.

Science says that in leadership roles, men and women aren't very different. As Catherine H. Tinsley and Robin J. Ely wrote in "What Most People Get Wrong About Men and Women," while there's wide variation among women and among men, meta-analyses show that, on average, the sexes are far more similar in their inclinations, attitudes, and skills than stereotypes would have us believe. The gender differences in workplace settings are not rooted in fixed gender traits but in "organizational structures, company practices, and patterns of interaction that position men and women differently, creating systematically different experiences for them. When facing dissimilar circumstances, people respond differently— not because of their sex but because of their situations."

It's a common belief that women are more committed to family than are men. Research, the authors say, does not support that idea. In a study of Harvard Business School graduates that one of the authors conducted, nearly every respondent, regardless of gender, placed a higher value on their families than on their work. While men's and women's desires and challenges about work/family balance were remarkably similar, the difference was in how their managers treated them at work. Fathers were assumed to be able to maintain a busy schedule, while mothers were assumed to be wanting and needing more support and less demanding duties. Such preconceptions led to a self-fulfilling prophecy: Fathers stayed at work while mothers dropped out.

When managers see differing success rates of women and men, or in behaviors that are critical to effectiveness, instead of assuming the gap is innate they can try to understand the organizational conditions that might be responsible. As the authors wrote, "Seriously investigating the context that gives rise to differential patterns in the way men and women experience the workplace—and intervening accordingly—can help companies chart a path to gender parity."[3]

Employee Archetypes Re-Invented

Traditional employee archetypes are widely used to further pigeonhole employees, primarily with a goal of achieving far better returns on human capital and increased productivity. All of these motivators are company centric and rarely give us much real insight as to what needs to be done in order to achieve a cultural transformation of happiness.

But if approached the right way, employee archetypes can be very useful in tailoring your survey questions to the personality of the employee.

In order to do a personification right we need to begin with an *employee-centric motivation*. In other words, we need to do all of this categorization with the goal of improving the quality of life for our employees, partners, and customers. Remember, this is the ecosystem that must be served in order for us to achieve a cultural transformation of happiness.

Everyone within our ecosystem must be happy or no one can be happy.

Happy employees are not trading their life for cash. They are trading their life at work for a great experience that allows them to express their unique creativity in a mission that matters in a way that serves others.

The Philosophical Shift

Before you can begin to create a culture of happiness, you must convene your leadership, including your board of directors, as you must get an absolute commitment for the long-term requirements of an initiative that will become part of your enterprise DNA. Your board of directors and top leadership must agree to the enterprise benefits of a happy culture while being educated to the financial, innovation, and competitive benefits as well. In other words, you must begin with an absolute philosophical shift to the idea that you are going to make happiness an enterprise stated and supported priority.

The Belief Shift

While the philosophical shift speaks to your commitment to succeeding at cultural transformation, the belief shift memorializes your commitment to the idea that your employees are your customers. We have heard much yammer about the idea of the so-called internal customer, but I've frankly never seen that deployed with any sincerity. Happiness is an ecosystem that is delivered to your employees, customers, partners, and all other stake-holders. The value exchange is quite simple: all employees want the ability to be honored and respected while being involved in a mission that they believe in that is offering their own growth while serving others.

Take Action!

✓ The RealRatings system creates a score of two sets of numbers: Hatepoints and Lovepoints.

Hatepoints are measured across four negative experiences, from 1 (slight hate) to 4 (maximum hate).

Lovepoints are measured across four positive experiences, from 1 (slight love) to 4 (maximum love).

The RealRating is the total of Hatepoints subtracted from the Lovepoints.

✓ The RealRating represents the net employee experience (or NEX) by subtracting the hate points from the love points to produce a score. It's just as important to *remove those things your employees hate* as it is to *strengthen those things your employees love*. Both are equally important.

✓ When forming employee archetypes, be sure to avoid the common pitfalls of using generational or gender stereotypes. Age and gender are just two demographic data points among hundreds that make up who we are and our expectations. It's crazy to think that your age or gender alone is a predictor of anyone's approach to their job.

✓ Before you can begin to create a culture of happiness, you must convene your leadership, including your board of directors, as you must get an absolute commitment for the long-term requirements of an initiative that will become part of your enterprise DNA. You must adopt this resolution: "Everyone within our ecosystem must be happy or no one can be happy."

CHAPTER 5

The Eight Emphasis Archetypes

Emphasis archetypes, as I call them, place a higher emphasis on different aspects of their happiness at work. There are six positive emphasis archetypes and two negative ones. These emphasis archetypes include:

The Leader

The leader archetype enjoys taking on responsibility and seeks opportunities to manage subordinates. They know what they want and will make unilateral decisions quickly. They aren't looking for validation or friendship and will quickly pile on the hate if they feel bogged down by bureaucracy. Many CEOs and politicians are leader archetypes—but not all, so be careful about generalizations! Probably the most famous corporate leader in recent history was Jack Welch, who from 1981 to 2001 relentlessly expanded General Electric into a massive conglomerate.

The leader archetype can be any age, any race, any gender identification, any nation of origin.

A challenge with leaders is that they can be overbearing and they often expect everyone on the team to share their relentless urge to act, even if the action is ill-advised. And very often we see that multiple leaders in one organization can create friction, as with Steve Jobs's first tenure at Apple from 1976 to 1985, and they ended up firing him.

The Dealer

The dealer archetype expects to be treated with respect and have a voice, as do all archetypes. However, this person places an emphasis on the deal. The various elements of the deal include pay, benefits, career trajectory, and to a certain extent, job security. This archetype is pragmatic and thoughtful about evaluating the best possible business deal for themselves, and they tend to be a bit less loyal. They also tend to stay at jobs for shorter periods of time and can be swayed away from an existing job with a better deal offer.

The dealer archetype can be any age, any race, any gender identification, any nation of origin.

Remember, all four positive archetypes are good and that includes the dealer archetype. Many dealer archetypes transition into different archetypes when they really feel comfortable at their work and know that they have a career trajectory within a given organization.

The Homemaker

The homemaker archetype sees their work as an extension of their home, and they place an emphasis on the importance of relationships with their boss and coworkers. They don't like to be treated like an employee, but like a trusted friend with a special place in the family dynamic. They don't like legalistic or hierarchical management structures. These archetypes tend to stay at a job for long periods of time. They're not easily swayed away from an organization that treats them with love and respect. Money matters to them, as does it with all archetypes, but these individuals will place their work/home life balance over financial incentives.

The homemaker archetype can be any age, any race, any gender identification, any nation of origin.

These are the people who will famously spend half an hour chatting on the phone with the customer. At a company like Zappos, this is exactly what the leaders want from their sales reps! At Zappos, forming the bond with the customer is the key sales strategy. It makes sense, because sooner or later every human being on earth needs to buy shoes—so why not buy them from Zappos?

On the other hand, homemakers often lack the drive and sense of urgency that's required from a leader. They may seem willing to just "go with the flow," even when that leads to decline. They may also be resistant to change and frightened of disruption.

The Analytical

This person needs to know every detail of the product or service. They make very good accountants and consultants because they're dedicated to the details of any process. And to solve product problems, such as how to write software code, you must have an analytical on board.

The analytical can be any age, any race, any gender identification, any nation of origin.

Analyticals are very good at executing the plans and designs created by visionaries. When architect David Childs designed the new One World Trade Center in New York City, making it the tallest building in the United States, you can bet his company, the architectural firm Skidmore, Owings & Merrill, had armies of analytical engineers dedicated to ensuring his design would actually work.

The problem with the analytical in a leadership role is that they can succumb to the aptly named "analysis paralysis" and postpone making a decision until they have more information—but the problem is that for them, there's never enough information. They can be maddeningly averse to risk.

The Visionary

A common type in business, this is the person who can see and articulate a future condition, such as, "Every house ought to have a computer in it." (Several visionaries have said this, including Steve Jobs, Bill Gates, and Michael Dell.) They thrive on disruption and often enjoy causing it. They embrace risk. To be successful, they need to have great communication skills and be humble enough to surround themselves with people who can make their vision a reality.

In business partnerships, you'll often see that one person is the visionary (like Steve Jobs), while the other is analytical or a leader (Steve Wozniak). It's difficult to have more than one visionary at the helm of a company—which is why Paul McCartney and John Lennon were perhaps destined to split up after being business partners for roughly a dozen years.

The visionary can be any age, any race, any gender identification, any nation of origin.

The visionary can also be someone who sees their *own future* and strives to create it. For example, Mary Barra, whom I mentioned earlier in the book, clearly had a vision of her own success at General Motors as she rose, year after year, through the ranks. Other CEOs who began at the bottom of their company include Walmart CEO Doug McMillon, who loaded trucks at a Walmart distribution center as a teenager, and Planet Fitness CEO Chris Rondeau, who started as a front desk receptionist at his local Planet Fitness gym. They may not be visionaries who disrupt or reshape an industry, but they're clearly oriented to the future and are adept at navigating change.

Of course, there are shades and combinations of each. For example, Jeff Bezos is clearly a visionary, but to succeed he had some of the qualities of the leader and the analytical. A little bit of the homemaker wouldn't have hurt, but it's not his most salient quality.

The Performer

The performer archetype sees their work as being closely connected to their own personal self-esteem and identity. They wear the company logo on their lapel pen, and they're proud to be associated with a brand while delivering quality products and services in a humanistic way. They are extremely good at what they do, they see their work as the stage on which they perform, and they are highly motivated by recognition of the quality and creativity of their work.

The performer archetype can be any age, any race, any gender identification, any nation of origin.

The Victim

The first of the two negative archetypes, the victim archetype, assumes that the organization is taking advantage of them and expecting too much work for too little pay. The derogatory archetype typically also has problems with coworkers, as they believe that they are victims of a system that they can't win at. Oftentimes, this archetype will try to do the least amount of work or push work off to other employees with the idea that this is how they achieve financial justice.

Archetypes who see themselves as victims don't tend to thrive in happy organizations as they typically need a pain partner as a coworker to discuss daily grievances. Victim archetypes also tend to try to find ways to take advantage of the organization and coworkers and are sometimes referred to as leech archetypes.

The victim archetype can be any age, any race, any gender identification, any nation of origin.

Some victim archetypes can be rehabilitated to a state of happiness, although I find this behavioral habit is hard to break. These are not bad people; oftentimes they are individuals who have truly been victims in a work situation and they simply weren't able to let it go.

The Destroyer

Destroyers do not see themselves as victims. They're living on a different ethical planet than other law-abiding citizens. Many are just plain criminals.

At the upper levels of a company, where they have power, destroyers can do terrible damage. You know their names: Bernie Madoff, Stewart Parnell (Peanut Corporation of America), Kenneth Lay and Jeffrey Skilling (Enron), Allen Stanford (Stanford Financial Group), Dennis Kozlowski (Tyco International), and many more.

Sometimes leaders can't control their base impulses. At the end of 2019, McDonald's CEO Steve Easterbrook was fired for sexting with a subordinate in what the company said was a consensual relationship. "Given the values of the company, I agree with the board that it is time for me to move on," Easterbrook said at the time in an email to employees. He departed with the usual generous golden parachute, in this case worth $40 million.

But soon, the scandal got worse. In August 2020, McDonald's filed a lawsuit against Easterbrook, alleging that he had physical sexual relationships with three McDonald's employees in the year before he was fired and approved stock grants worth hundreds of thousands of dollars to one of those women. The company also claimed that he concealed evidence during its initial investigation, deleting emails from his phone. With these alleged new revelations, McDonald's argued it had cause to fire Easterbrook and that he should repay his severance package.

Easterbrook retorted that when the company negotiated his severance, they knew about the stock awards and had the information about his other relationships

In August 2021, more bad news erupted when a pension fund, an institutional investor, and an individual stockholder requested that a Delaware state court force McDonald's to share records related to the termination of Easterbrook as well as former human resources chief David Fairhurst. The stockholders argued the board should have led a thorough investigation of Easterbrook's behavior before granting his exit package.

And then investor Phyllis Gianotti sued McDonald's, alleging the chain breached its fiduciary duty by failing to curb incidents of racial discrimination, sexual harassment, and other misconduct. Gianotti argued that the company's law firm, Morgan Lewis, rushed its initial investigation, which concluded after eight days, of then-CEO Steve Easterbrook's inappropriate relationship with an employee. The suit also referenced previous complaints of racial discrimination and declines in the percent of Black executives at McDonald's.

"I'm lovin' it"? Maybe not so much![1]

Many Loves, Many Hates

While it's true that happy employees all want to go to a place of work where people respect them, acknowledge them, and help them grow, the six positive archetypes each view your company, and their work inside it, through their own individual lens. They literally see your organization differently from the others.

If asked to describe your company, the leader might say, "We move fast and break things. Nothing stands in our way!" Or if a leader is feeling less love, they might say, "We move too slowly. Our employees and board aren't motivated for success. They're all too timid."

The analytical might say, "We take great care to weigh each decision carefully in order to minimize risk and optimize our return on investment." Or if feeling less love, it might be, "Too many decisions are made without enough research. We fly by the seat of our pants and are taking too many risks."

The homemaker might say, "This is a wonderful company to work for! Everyone is so easygoing and supportive." Or if feeling less love, "I feel too much pressure here. It's like a rat race. This company has no soul. Everyone is consumed by our insatiable drive for profits."

The visionary might say, "We represent the future! We aim to disrupt the status quo and show the world what it's never seen before." On the negative side, it might be, "This company is hopelessly stuck in the mud. We're doing the same old thing over and over again."

And guess what? They could all be talking about the same company!

Oh, and the destroyer? It might very well be that the destroyer, in seeking to preserve his meal ticket, will simply lie and claim to love everything about the company.

That raises the important question about how truthful employees will be when responding to any survey. We'll discuss that in the pages ahead, but the short answer is twofold:

1. The RealRatings system *requires* the respondent to say what they hate about the company, as well as what they love. Neutral or "no opinion" responses are not accepted.
2. The willingness of an employee to say something negative about the company is a direct reflection of the culture of the organization, and the culture is under the control of the CEO. If the employee works in a culture of fear, then he or she will feel as though they have no choice but to speak falsehoods to authority. If the employee works in a culture of happiness and trust, then he or she will feel comfortable in offering constructive criticism.

The critically important fact that most employee surveys ignore, and cannot measure, is that *each archetype has a different set of loves and hates.* The chatty coworker will be hated by the leader and loved by the home-maker. The impulsive manager will be hated by the analytical, who wants to spend time gathering information, but loved by the leader, who wants to waste no time. The "mad scientist" in R&D who's always cooking up crazy ideas will be loved by the visionary, but might be disliked by his analytical budget director, who sees nothing but money going out the window.

This is why the wise CEO who leads a dynamic organization and uses the RealRatings system will accept the fact that some tension among many diverse employees is to be expected. The people in marketing may have criticisms of the people in sales, and the salespeople may have issues with the people in fulfillment or quality control. A bit of healthy competition is good, as long as the company culture is one of respect, shared goals, and happiness.

You Need Just the Right Mix

Among the six healthy archetypes in a positive company culture there will always be common ground. The leader will respect the homemaker's good heart. The visionary will appreciate the analytical's attention to detail. The homemaker will moderate the visionary's single-mindedness.

The victim? A challenge for any manager. Some can be brought around to be positive contributors.

The destroyer? Nothing positive here. Get rid of them as soon as you can.

The fact is that every large organization needs a mix of all six positive types because they each have something to offer. In addition, a company with an imbalance will not perform well. If there are too many leaders with few analyticals to support them, what the leaders seek to accomplish may run off the rails. If there's a strong visionary with no homemakers to smooth out the rough edges, the visionary may have trouble keeping loyal employees because they'll get fed up with his or her lofty head-in-the-clouds attitude. And every company needs a few performers to act as cheerleaders and brand ambassadors.

You Need Six Different Surveys

Okay, I know what you're thinking:

"As if we haven't got enough to do in trying to run our business, you're saying we need multiple employee surveys? Are you joking?"

No, I'm not joking. But the secret is that it's much easier than you think.

Your employees will take their RealRatings survey online, either on the company's internet or through a secure portal. If your employees are suspicious about being identified, then set up a common computer terminal in the break room or an unused office and tell them to use that one. But hopefully your organization has a sufficient level of trust so that will not be necessary.

The first question will serve to direct or sort the employee into one of the six archetypes. If necessary, a series of semiredundant questions can be asked to make a more secure determination. The victim and destroyer will probably lie, which underscores the importance of *personal contact* between managers and employees, which is the most effective way to uncover these negative types.

The first question could be:

1. I work at ABC Company because:
   A. ABC Company is driven to move fast and get the job done for our customers.
   B. ABC Company is a friendly, congenial place to work, almost like a second home.
   C. ABC Company values accuracy and appreciates my attention to detail.
   D. ABC Company has a vision for innovation and transforming our marketplace.

E. ABC Company pays me to do my job. I'd be happy to work anywhere.

F. ABC Company gives me a sense of pride when I'm in the community.

Because this is just a qualifying round, the respondent can be asked to rank the choices from 1 to 6, using all six numbers. This will ensure one top choice.

Based on their top choice, or choices if more than one qualifying question is used, the respondent is then presented with one of six different surveys. This is a simple function of a decision tree, which is a flowchart-like structure in which each internal node represents a test on an attribute (such as whether a coin flip comes up heads or tails), each branch represents the outcome of the test, and each leaf node represents a class label (decision taken after computing all attributes).

The survey presented to leaders will be different from the survey presented to homemakers, analyticals, visionaries, and victims. The survey presented to leaders will focus not only on the ubiquitous questions of everyday company operations, but on questions designed to measure to what extent the company scored love points and/or hate points based on the specific expectations of leaders. Likewise for the other four archetypes; each will receive their own customized survey designed to measure how well the company met their expectations.

After the initial qualifying question or questions, each respondent is presented with the survey appropriate for them. They are asked to answer two sets of questions. There should be no more than five in each set, for a maximum number of questions set at 10, plus the initial qualifying question.

Survey for the Leader

In the first set of five questions, the leader respondent is asked about what she loved about her work. In the second set of five questions, she's asked about what she dislikes. We *want her* to tell us something she hated. The love-hate sequence goes like this:

1. Using the scale of 1 (slight love), 2 (some love), 3 (love), or 4 (maximum love), please indicate your level of *happiness* with the following five job factors:
   A. The pace of work and your workload.
   B. The support you receive from your direct superior.
   C. The hours you work.
   D. The clarity of direction you receive.
   E. The tools and training you have to help you do your job.
2. Using the scale of 1 (slight hate), 2 (some hate), 3 (hate), or 4 (maximum hate), please indicate your level of *dissatisfaction* with the following five job factors:
   A. The level of cooperation among your team members.
   B. Your personal attachment to the products we make.
   C. How often you're asked for your ideas and input.
   D. How much your direct superior "has your back" and sees your point of view.
   E. The overall direction of the company and its products.

As you can see, the questions presented in the two parts are similar but not exactly the same. The reason we ask specifically for what the employee hates is to give the employee "permission" to express their true feelings. We're asking them what they don't like about their experience, and we want them to tell us.

Also note that these questions are particularly relevant to the values and expectations of a leader. This employee knows what he or she wants to accomplish and is not as "big picture" oriented as the visionary. Nor are they as concerned with being friends, like the homemaker, or of the minutiae of every detail, like the analytical employee.

There is one more very important caveat: Because this person is a leader, we should expect a low level of "love." They are very pragmatic and tend to check their feelings at the door each morning. With leaders, you want to eliminate hate points as much as possible, and then settle for a minimally positive set of love points.

Survey for the Homemaker

Now let's take a look at the same survey when presented to an homemaker. You will see that some of the questions are the same (functioning as a control set) while others are tailored for the homemaker's expectations:

1. Using the scale of 1 (slight love), 2 (some love), 3 (love), or 4 (maximum love), please indicate your level of *happiness* with the following five job factors:
   A. The pace of work and your workload.
   B. The support you receive from your direct superior.
   C. Your opportunities to bond with your colleagues.
   D. The overall level of happiness you experience within the organization.
   E. Compliance by the company with laws regarding sexual or other harassment.
2. Using the scale of 1 (slight hate), 2 (some hate), 3 (hate), or 4 (maximum hate), please indicate your level of *dissatisfaction* with the following five job factors:
   A. The level of cooperation among your team members.
   B. Your comfort level with bringing a complaint to your supervisor.
   C. How often you're asked for your ideas and input.
   D. The amount of professional respect you receive.
   E. How quickly your supervisor answers a question.

With a homemaker, you especially want to pay attention to the responses that relate to how well respected they feel, because this is likely to be the most important part of the experience for them.

Again, these are just hypothetical, sample questions. The questions you ask need to be tailored specifically for your business environment and employees. A survey for an online business will be very different, as will a hotel or a restaurant. The point is that the RealRatings survey will provide you with highly specific, actionable information about what your employees love and hate *according to their individual expectations.* The slight redundancy of the love/hate questions will provide a verification of veracity (or not); for example, if a leader expresses very *low* love for the support she receives from her direct superior (question 1-B), then you should expect her to express a correspondingly high level of hate for how much her direct superior "has her back" and sees her point of view (question 2-D).

In this book, I've presented eight employee archetypes. This is just the most basic breakdown. In practice, your business could create as many employee archetypes as you believe to be necessary. If it were relevant, you could add demographic qualifiers like age, but only if you're certain that different age groups have different expectations—for instance, if they want different compensation packages. The trick is to quickly move them through the qualifying phase before they get bored and want to either abandon or shortcut the survey.

Before the digital age, producing this level of agility and granularity would have been impossible. The data would have been too much to process, and the "decision tree" feature, where the respondent is instantly characterized according to his or her archetype, didn't exist. Today, with our powerful databases and processing tools, it will be easy to construct a RealRatings survey system that presents to each respondent a survey that is concise and tailored precisely to their expectations.

Take Action!

✓ Emphasis archetypes recognize differences in employee
happiness at work. There are six positive emphasis
archetypes:

> The Leader
> The Dealer
> The Homemaker
> The Analytical
> The Visionary
> The Performer

And two negative archetypes:

> The Victim
> The Destroyer

✓ Each archetype views your company and their work
inside it through their own individual lens. They literally
see your organization differently from the others.

✓ Each archetype has a different set of loves and hates,
which may switch 180 degrees from one to another.

✓ When crafting employee surveys, you must steer
each archetype to the survey tailored for them.
For example, a Leader should not receive the same
survey as a Homemaker.

CHAPTER 6

Creating the Employee Persona

It's an axiom of human resources and employee management that if you hire the right person for the job, then that person has a much better chance of long-term success and will be happier in their work than someone who was shoehorned into the job because the company needed to fill the position quickly.

The rule has been codified into the saying, "hire slow, fire fast."

Let's look at the first part, "hire slow."

Organizations hire new people for two reasons:

1. To replace someone who's leaving.
2. To recruit someone to fill a new position for the first time.

In the first case—replacement—there are three scenarios. The first is that the person was doing a bad job and you're firing them. The second is that the person was doing a mediocre job, but because of seniority or because the person was well-liked, they were never fired. Perhaps now they're retiring or relocating. The third scenario is that the person was doing a very good job but is leaving due to retirement or a better opportunity elsewhere.

In the first two scenarios, you want to hire someone who will do the job *differently* than the previous employee. You want them to be *better,* whatever that means.

In the third scenario, you want to find someone who can meet the high standards set by the person who's departing, and be ready to meet future challenges.

In every scenario, you need to hire someone *with intention*, meaning you have a clear set of expectations. Because the job already exists, and has a history, it may seem like an easy task to find a candidate you can quickly "plug into" the role. The pressure to do this can increase if the person leaving was a true value creator and the company may suffer if the position is vacant. How many times have leaders panicked because a key team member has given their two-week notice and they believe the company will be crippled unless a new person is quickly found?

But a fast hire often leads to failure and separation. According to a 2017 CareerBuilder Survey, 74 percent of employers say they have hired the wrong person for a position. Why did they do this? According to the survey, 35 percent knew the candidate didn't have all the needed skills but felt they could learn quickly; 32 percent took a chance on a nice person; 30 percent felt pressured to fill the role quickly; and 29 percent focused on skills and not attitude. (Some employers provided more than one reason.)[1]

The cost of a "bad hire" can be significant. The U.S. Department of Labor estimates the average cost of a bad hiring decision is 30 percent or more of the individual's first-year expected earnings. If you take an employee with an annual income of $90,000, the cost to the organization can be $30,000. Others argue that when you add up all the costs, it's actually greater:

- Recruitment advertising fees and/or agency costs.
- Hours spent reviewing résumés and interviewing candidates.
- Time and expenses associated with onboarding and training the new employee.

- Time and expenses spent managing poor performance and diminished productivity.
- Impact of stress on team morale.
- Risk of poor customer service and damage to brand.
- Increased risk of legal fees from claims of unlawful termination or discrimination.

Part of the problem is that many managers who need to hire for their teams are not trained interviewers. They may be good at marketing or finance or whatever they do, but they're not good at hiring. A CareerBuilder survey found that 22 percent—nearly one in five—of managers admitted they lacked the training to effectively interview and hire people.[2]

Hiring is a skill like any other, and it needs to be learned.

In an effort to make the hiring process more efficient and more likely to produce a positive outcome, many companies are producing employee personas.

If this sounds familiar, it may be because for many years companies have created customer personas to serve as target customers for products either in development or being newly marketed. Marketing and product development personas tend to work very well. Brands develop their ideal customer persona or avatar—which can be a very detailed description—and then design a product for that customer. This makes sense because there are over 7 billion people living on this planet, and most companies have no choice but to carefully identify the subset of people who might buy their product. They cannot afford to waste time and money trying to sell a product to someone who will never buy it.

Teena, Antonella, and Jack

For example, one of the very first modern customer personas was created by *Seventeen* magazine the year 1950. Based on survey data from teenage girls and their mothers during the mid-1940s, the publisher created a persona named Teena. Here's how they described Teena:

Teena the High School Girl has a peck of problems. She's what older folks call an awkward adolescent— too tall, too plump, too shy—a little too much of a lot of little things. But they're big things to Teena. And though she doesn't always take her troubles to her mother, Teena writes her favorite magazine for the tip-off on the clothes she wears, the food she eats, the lipstick she wields, the room she bunks in, the budget she keeps, the boy she has a crush on.[3]

It was a very simple matter for an editor to ask a writer: "Will this article appeal to Teena?"

In 2008, the Ford Motor Company was developing a concept car named the Ford Verve, which became the sixth-generation Ford Fiesta, which had been sold in Europe since 1976 and which the company eventually introduced in the United States in 2010. The design of the Verve was spearheaded not by engineers but by marketers, who first created the target customer for the car. The engineers then built the car to fit the needs and aspirations of the customer—a personification of a profile that was created on the basis of demographic research about the target market for the Ford Fiesta.

They gave her a name: Antonella. She was 28 years old and a resident of Rome, Italy. While not wealthy, her life was focused on friends and fun, clubbing and parties. She was a sophisticated version of a type the Ford designers called the "fun-seeker."

Antonella cared more about the design and function of her telephone than that of her car. The car's central panel controls operating the audio and air-conditioning systems were inspired by those of a cellphone. The shape of the Verve's instrument cluster pods were meant to mirror the kind of glasses she would wear, and designers working on the Fiesta referred to the shape as "Antonella's glasses."

While Antonella happened to live in Rome, Ford's goal in using fictional characters was that they would help produce cars that transcended national traits and were instead built around international, psychological archetypes. "There are fun-seekers in London and Cleveland," said Moray Callum, executive director of Ford America's design program.

But the image of the fun-seeker became more vivid when set in Rome. "In Rome there are lots of small cars," Murat Yalman, Ford's director of global advanced product strategy, told the *New York Times*. "They are always dodging each other. So a car there has to be nimble and it has to look the part. Romans have been conscious of how their vehicles look all the way back to Caesar. Every little crease of their toga has to be just right."

Internally, the use of a customer persona gives everyone on the design team a single target to shoot for. "Invented characters get everyone on the same page," said Callum. "Personalizing gives context to the information we have. Sometimes the target demographics are difficult to relate to by, say, a 35-year-old male designer."[4]

With Antonella, all the designer needs to do is ask, "Would this feature of the car appeal to Antonella?"

Ford has used many fictional personas when designing vehicles. Natasha, who resembled Audrey Hepburn, was the customer persona for the luxury Lincoln. The Ford Transit Connect van was created around Ashley, a "cool mom." The driver of the Ford Taurus was Jack, "the life of the party." They all gave the designers guidance and an architecture for making choices.

Craft Your Candidate Persona

In today's hypercompetitive market, it's become imperative that you know your customer and design your product to make them deliriously happy. And it's not just about increasing happiness; it's also about decreasing unhappiness. My best-selling book *What Customers Hate* reveals that by reducing what customers *hate* about your product or service, you'll help them to *love it more* and inoculate your brand against the attacks of competitors.

The same principle applies when selling your company to another type of "customer"—prospective employees. You want the process to be as efficient as possible and get the candidate who's a perfect fit as quickly as possible. You want the hate points on both sides to be minimal and the love points to be at their maximum.

In order to find the best possible job candidate—the person whose interaction with the company will produce the most love points and fewest hate points—the world's best companies are using the concept of the customer persona to create job candidate personas.

A job candidate persona is a semifictional representation of your ideal job candidate. Hiring professionals use industry research, hiring trends, and anecdotal evidence to truly describe and visualize their ideal candidate. The character is derived from data surrounding work history, skills, qualifications, and education. These are the quantitative aspects. The most effective candidate personas go beyond information found within a résumé and explore qualitative traits that make someone the perfect hire. This often includes personality traits, career goals, soft skills, and sometimes even employment preferences.

Before we go any further, there's one huge difference between a customer persona and a candidate persona. Unlike the customer persona, the candidate persona must *never* include specifications that would represent discrimination in hiring.

Under the laws enforced by the US Equal Employment Opportunity Commission (EEOC), it is illegal to discriminate against someone (applicant or employee) because of that person's race, color, religion, sex (including gender identity, sexual orientation, and pregnancy), national origin, age (40 or older), disability, or genetic information.

These metrics cannot be a part of your candidate persona.

Instead, the candidate persona must focus on two sets of information:

1. The quantitative elements that include things like education, job experience, and qualifications.
2. The quantitative elements that include things like identification with the organization's mission, willingness to innovate, desire to be a team player, and basic work ethic.

If you want to give your candidate persona a name, you should use one that's "unisex" or gender-neutral, such as Robin, Pat, Kim, or Blake.

Okay, having gotten that piece of business out of the way, how do you go about creating a candidate persona?

First, let's consider the scenario where you're looking to fill an existing position. In this case, it's likely that the position will have some generic industry aspects and some aspects that are specific to your company. For example, if you're looking for a chief information security officer (CISO), this is a position found within many large companies. Your candidate will have some basic qualifications common to the job, but you'll also be looking for your own specific requirements.

The process of candidate persona creation can be broken down into three steps: collecting data, identifying common data points between successful candidates, and then defining the persona.

1. Compile Data

Compile data surrounding previously successful hires and placements in your own company (internal) as well as at other companies in your industry (external). On the external side, you need to see the same data your candidate will see when they do their job search.

Recruiters can uncover internal information in a number of different ways, but we suggest you start by interviewing current employees. For optimal results, consider focusing your research on top performers within a specific position or department.

For example, say you're looking to hire a marketing manager. Start by looking at the résumés of marketing managers you've successfully placed in the past and the performance data of top-tier marketing managers. Then, interview internal and external professionals who currently work in that role to understand what qualities make them successful. To take it a step further, you can gather anecdotal evidence or commentary by consulting other recruiters and hiring managers who have hired marketing managers in the past.

Remember that while personas are distilled down to a single character, in reality, they are a composite of many different people. That said, aim to gather as much information as possible regarding the position. The more data you have to work with, the more detailed your personas will be.

Here are key data points to prioritize, many of which can already be found in your candidate or recruiting database. They are divided into quantitative attributes and qualitative attributes.

Quantitative

- **Demographic information.** Location, current job title, income expectation.
- **Background.** Educational and professional history.
- **Qualifications.** Required or preferred skills, certifications, coursework, etc.

Qualitative

- **Goals.** What kind of career do they want to build? Where do they want to be in five years?
- **Personal attributes.** Personality characteristics, strengths, weaknesses, interests, and fears.
- **Objections.** What would cause a candidate to not want to work for a company? What aspects of a company's brand, culture or hiring process would cause them to lose interest?
- **Web activity.** Where do they spend time on the internet? Identify which online platforms they utilize for leisure, for networking and of course, where they look for jobs.

2. Add Your Internal Requirements

In Step 1, you surveyed as many sources as possible, both internal and external. This gave you a generic data set describing the position in general—for example, marketing managers in your industry. These attributes are what you'll find in the average marketing manager. It's what most companies will be looking for.

Within your industry, your company will have its own personality, culture, and goals. Your marketing manager will work under conditions that are unique to you. Perhaps you have an aggressive social media presence, or as a marketing strategy your company sponsors sports teams or underwrites charitable programs in developing nations. Therefore, you'll need someone with experience or qualifications in those areas.

The goal is to develop the qualities and characteristics that make up the ideal candidate for the position (or positions) you're trying to fill. It may help to ask yourself the following questions:

- What skills must the candidate persona absolutely have?
- Do successful candidates often share common job or career-specific experiences?
- What motivates the candidate persona to succeed in our company?
- Where does the candidate see themselves in five years? Is there a path for advancement in our company, or will the employee eventually jump ship for a promotion elsewhere?
- What is the candidate persona looking for in their work environment? Are things like paid maternity and paternity leave important to them?
- Where does our candidate persona search for jobs? Do we need to hire a headhunter to identify the candidate(s) who closely match our persona?
- What's the command structure for this job? To whom will the employee report, and who will report to the employee, if anyone? Do we need a certain personality type to succeed?

This last question is particularly on point. Does the position require, or would be best suited for, a leader, dealer, homemaker, analytical, visionary, performer? The answers to these questions will help you define the candidate persona who will best meet your needs for the role.

3. Assemble and Launch the Persona

After collecting and analyzing your data, it's time to assemble your candidate persona. Give them a name—say, Blake. But no other EEOC-proscribed demographic information. You'll simply say:

Blake has these attributes:
    Then you list them.

BLAKE

    It's important to remember that your end goal should not be an external job description, but rather a detailed internal description of your ideal candidate. But it will inform the job description that you'll post and candidates will see. The job description is likely to be one of the first touchpoints they have with your company, which is why it's crucial to write a job description that accurately describes your specific candidate persona. This will help candidates better understand what your company is looking for, allowing them to determine whether they see themselves as a match for the role before applying. This will, in turn, ensure that candidates who apply for the role will be closely matched (aside from the flaky people who apply to any job, regardless of their qualifications!), saving you time reviewing fewer unqualified applications.

Pursuing Diversity

Earlier in this chapter I advised that demographic information about EEOC-proscribed attributes had no place in your candidate persona. Title VII of the Civil Rights Act—which every HR manager knows by heart—is the federal law that prohibits employers from discriminating against their employees based on race, color, national origin, gender, and religion. These prohibitions apply to recruiting, hiring, promoting, transferring, training, disciplining, discharging, assigning work, measuring performance, and/or providing benefits. Under this statute, employers may not consider race, color, gender, or any other protected group when making any type of employment decision.

What can you do if you want to deliberately pursue a program of workplace diversity? That's a difficult question.

According to guidance issued by the EEOC (and based on the U.S. Supreme Court's *United Steelworkers of America, AFL-CIO-CLC v. Weber* decision), a voluntary affirmative action program stands on solid legal ground if (1) an analysis reveals that existing or contemplated employment practices are likely to cause an actual or potential adverse impact; (2) a comparison between the employer's workforce and the appropriate labor pool reveals that it is necessary to correct the effects of previous discriminatory practices; and (3) a limited labor pool of qualified minorities and women for employment or promotional opportunities exists due to historical restrictions by employers, labor organizations, or others.[5]

But most companies cannot demonstrate a voluntary affirmative action program.

Except in a very limited number of circumstances, a decision not to hire someone because of any Title VII classifications constitutes discrimination and a possible lawsuit. This means that if you receive two applications for a job opening, one from a White man and one from a Hispanic woman, you cannot choose to hire the woman solely because you want to increase the number of women and people of color in your workplace.

You cannot include limitations, specifications, or discriminatory language in your outward-facing job advertisement, nor should you in your internal candidate persona. An employer who wants to hire more women may be tempted to simply include that in the job posting: "Software company seeks female developer." This will get you in trouble. Many state laws prohibit job advertisements that include limitations, specifications, or discrimination based on any of the Title VII classifications.

You could assert that your workplace is diverse. In your job listing, you could say something like, "All interested individuals, including people of all races and national origin, people of all ages, people of all religions, people with or without disabilities, and/or people with any gender identity and sexual orientation, are urged to apply."

To protect yourself against claims of discrimination while hiring, document every part of the hiring process. This includes keeping copies of the job posting, any résumés or applications the company received in response to the posting, and the notes taken by all interviewers.

If you have the slightest concern about your company's hiring policies or procedures, be sure to consult a qualified employment and labor attorney.

Take Action!

- ✓ In order to find the best possible job candidate—the person whose interaction with the company will produce the most love points and fewest hate points—use the concept of the customer persona to create job candidate personas.
- ✓ Unlike the customer persona, the candidate persona must *never* include specifications that would represent discrimination in hiring. Under the laws enforced by the U.S. EEOC, it is illegal to discriminate against someone (applicant or employee) because of that person's race, color, religion, sex (including gender identity, sexual

orientation, and pregnancy), national origin, age (40 or older), disability, or genetic information. These metrics cannot be a part of your candidate persona.

✓ The process of candidate persona creation can be broken down into three steps:

1. Compile data surrounding previously successful hires and placements in your own company (internal) as well as at other companies in your industry (external).

2. Add your internal requirements and develop the qualities and characteristics that make up the ideal candidate for the position (or positions) you're trying to fill.

3. Assemble and launch the persona. Your end goal should not be an external job description, but rather a detailed internal description of your ideal candidate.

✓ An overt attempt to pursue employee diversity may violate the law. In your job listing, you could say something like, "All interested individuals, including people of all races and national origin, people of all ages, people of all religions, people with or without disabilities, and/or people with any gender identity and sexual orientation, are urged to apply." If you have the slightest concern about your company's hiring policies or procedures, be sure to consult a qualified employment and labor attorney.

CHAPTER 7

Designing the Happy Job

In order to have happy employees, it stands to reason that you should have "happy jobs." After all, if a role is a "miserable job," then it's hard to see how anyone could be happy doing it. This suggests two interesting thoughts to ponder. Namely:

1. There are some jobs that many people would hate to do while others find very enjoyable. For example, consider Carlos Barrios Orta, a former accountant turned official Mexico City sewer diver. The *Washington Post* detailed his workday spent immersed in "garbage, bacteria, excrement, dead animals—even the occasional murder victim." On a typical day he'd squeeze himself into a rubber diving suit, pull on an 18-pound helmet that made him look like an astronaut, then lower himself into the filthy water, which looked like "some cauldron of rancid beef stew." His workstation was a massive drain underneath the streets of Mexico City, where the smell of human waste and rotting trash was so strong it was hard for a visitor not to vomit. But Barrios, one of four divers who maintained the 600 miles of sewers and pipes beneath the biggest city in North America, calmly did his job, which was to keep the pumps and sewers clear of

debris. He loved his job and said he'd never go back to being an accountant.[1]

2. There are some jobs that you'd think would be amazingly rewarding but which create misery from the conditions under which people are forced to work. For example, you'd think that surgeons would lead very satisfying lives because they're in the business of healing people. That may be true, but among many surgeons, job burnout is a serious issue. Forty percent of the 7,905 surgeons who responded to a June 2008 survey commissioned by the American College of Surgeons for a study led by researchers from Johns Hopkins University School of Medicine and the Mayo Clinic said they were burned out. Nine percent reported having made a major medical mistake in the previous three months, and these mistakes were partially attributable to job burnout.

Researchers asked a variety of questions, including queries that rated three elements of burnout—emotional exhaustion, depersonalization, and personal accomplishment—and others that screened for depression. According to the report entitled, "Burned Out, Depressed Surgeons More Likely to Commit More Major Medical Errors," each one-point increase on a scale that measured depersonalization—a feeling of withdrawal or of treating patients as objects rather than as human beings—was associated with an 11 percent increase in the likelihood of reporting an error. Each one-point increase on a scale measuring emotional exhaustion was associated with a 5 percent increase.

"People have talked about fatigue and long working hours, but our results indicate that the dominant contributors to self-reported medical errors are burnout and depression," said Charles M. Balch, MD, a professor of surgery at the Johns Hopkins University School of Medicine and one of the study's leaders.[2]

The Covid-19 pandemic created stressful working conditions for healthcare providers. In a national survey of 20,947 doctors and others working in health care during the pandemic, 38 percent reported anxiety or depression, 43 percent suffered from work overload, and 49 percent had experienced burnout.

Stress scores were highest among nursing assistants, medical assistants, social workers, and inpatient workers (nurses, respiratory therapists, nursing assistants and housekeepers) as well as among women, Black, and Latinx health care workers.

But here's an interesting twist: the odds of burnout were 40 percent lower in those who felt valued by their organizations, which was 46 percent of respondents.[3]

Evidently, a person's happiness at work depends on two things: if the person enjoys the work itself, and if the work is done in an environment that does not put excessive pressure, physical and mental, on the worker. Even a fulfilling job, such as healing other people, can become unpleasant when the stress and pressure pile up.

Maslow's Hierarchy of Needs

This brings to mind the "hierarchy of needs," first proposed by American Abraham Maslow in his 1943 paper "A Theory of Human Motivation" in the journal *Psychological Review.* He proposed that in our life on earth, we humans have the opportunity to not merely survive but to ascend in our development through five stages. The hierarchy of needs is often portrayed in the shape of a pyramid, with the largest, most fundamental needs at the bottom, and then going up through the five layers to the top. The five needs, which are normally satisfied in ascending order, are:

1. **Physiological.** The basic needs of life: food, water, shelter, reproduction, sleep.
2. **Safety.** This includes physical, emotional, and financial security.
3. **Love and social belonging.** Being part of a family or group and being loved by another.
4. **Self-actualization.** "What a person *can* be, they *must* be," forms the basis of the perceived need for the realization of one's

full potential. Maslow describes this as the desire to accomplish everything that one can, to become the most that one can be.

5. **Transcendence and spirituality.** Maslow defined it as, "The very highest and most inclusive or holistic levels of human consciousness, behaving and relating, as ends rather than means, to oneself, to significant others, to human beings in general, to other species, to nature, and to the cosmos."

You may not expect your job as an insurance adjuster (for example) to get you to level 5, but it certainly ought to get you to level 3, and hopefully level 4. The fact is that people who are stuck at levels 1 or 2—and in the United States there are many millions of them—are not going to feel happy about their place in life. To be at level 2 and be happy, you need to *see a bright future.* You need to be able to embrace your temporary discomfort because you believe life will get better.

As The Good Jobs Institute pointed out, you can say that a "good job" provides two levels of needs:

- **Basic needs comprise these four:** Pay and benefits, schedules, career path, and security and safety.
- **Higher needs comprise these five:** Meaningfulness, personal growth, belonging, achievement, and recognition.

The company's "Good Jobs Strategy" consists of four components surrounding the center component, which is "Invest in people." These four components are:

1. **Focus and simplify.** Simplify operations in a way that maximizes value for customers and improves employee productivity and motivation.
2. **Standardize and empower.** With employee input, standardize routine processes while empowering employees to improve those standards. Employees can also make decisions that improve customer service and reduce cost.

3. **Cross-train.** Build flexibility to meet fluctuating customer demand by cross-training employees.

4. **Operate with slack.** Staff units with more hours of labor than the expected workload. This will help the company meet peak customer demand and give employees time to perform their tasks with confidence.

In the center is "Invest in people." Companies that follow the Good Jobs Strategy invest in people in a way that combines with operations to create a virtuous cycle. Investment in people includes recruiting, training, establishing clear career paths, creating high performance standards, and offering fair wages and predictable schedules.

Finding Meaning in Work

You'll recall the Happy Work formula:

$$Work + Recreation + Meaning = Happy Work$$

We've defined "work" and "recreation," and since they're relatively straightforward, simple terms, there's no need to further define their meanings.

The word "meaning" is trickier. It can suggest different things to different people. For the sake of simplicity, let's stick with the definition we introduced in Chapter 2, which says that "meaning" is the deep personal satisfaction we get when we make something or provide a service that contributes to our culture or improves the lives of others.

This is all well and good, but when you're talking about an organization of five, or fifty, or five thousand people, it's very important that everyone on the team shares the same idea of what gives them meaning at work. This is not a trivial issue; many companies have been destroyed because leaders could not agree on what they personally saw as providing meaning to their work.

Here's where it gets complicated, but in a way that can be very useful for leadership.

Mission Statements

Every organization has (or should have!) an overall mission statement, as well as various other statements such as vision and values. The mission statement is defined as an action-based declaration of the purpose of an organization and how they serve their customers. This sometimes includes a description of the company, what it does, and its objectives. It's an expression, made by its leaders and stakeholders, of their desires and intent for the organization. The purpose is to communicate the organization's purpose and direction to its employees, customers, vendors, and other stakeholders.

Some mission statements are very simple:

- "Spread ideas." —TED
- "To put people at the center of enterprise software." —Workday
- "To help bring creative projects to life." —Kickstarter
- "To spread the power of optimism." —Life Is Good

You'll notice that even these short mission statements each contain an action verb and a goal. They express what the organization does on a daily basis.

Some mission statements are very detailed:

- "To provide superior quality healthcare services that: PATIENTS recommend to family and friends, PHYSICIANS prefer for their patients, PURCHASERS select for their clients, EMPLOYEES are proud of, and INVESTORS seek for long-term returns." —Universal Health Services, Inc.

The UHS mission statement encompasses its universe of stakeholders and the variety of positive actions they will take as the result of the company's activities.

Many organizations also have a **vision statement**. This typically describes the world the organization is trying to create or is striving for. It's what they want the future to look like. For example:

- "A just world without poverty." —Oxfam
- "We're in business to save our home planet." —Patagonia

While the line between mission statements and vision statements can be blurry, the goal of both is twofold:

1. To align leaders, employees, investors, and other stakeholders in the same direction. To get everyone on the team on the same page.
2. To communicate to customers the intention and goals of the company, because this may influence their buying decision (such as in the case of Patagonia, above).

Many organizations also have **statements of values**. These describe how the organization intends to move forward in terms of its ethics and business practices. In theory, all values statements could be identical and extol the virtues of honesty and integrity. But each organization has their own way of saying it. Many are expressed in terms of a list or bullet points, such as this one from Marriott International, Inc.:

- We Put People First
- We Pursue Excellence
- We Embrace Change
- We Act with Integrity
- We Serve Our World

When onboarding a new hire, it's important to make clear to the person why the company does what it does. It may be self-evident (Marriott is a hotel chain, right?) but people enter organizations for all sorts of reasons and with all sorts of personal baggage. Some want a job—*any* job—and don't care what they do as long as they get a paycheck. Others might view the position as the first step in a long career in the industry. When approaching their new job, employees will absorb all the cues and clues they get from their environment: the behavior of their bosses and peers, the company's attitude toward its customers, the stated mission, vision, and values. How they behave will reflect these combined influences.

Ideally, the happy worker will want to be in the specific job they have with the specific company. But at least until the Great Resignation, many workers were willing to endure jobs for which they had little affection. They were willing to be unhappy in return for their paycheck. That's changing. Covid-19 was like a bucket of cold water dumped on their heads, jolting them into awareness. When people went to work, or were asked to come back to work, they asked themselves, "What am I doing this for?"

Making It Personal

In a very small company, where everyone knows everyone else and there's lots of job sharing, having an overall mission statement may be enough. A small staff can readily discuss their goals and work out how they want to move ahead, and the meaning of a particular role can be very clear to the person doing it. But in a large organization with multiple departments and workers who may not have contact with each other, it's often necessary to have a mission statement for each department. This is because it can be difficult for each employee to see how their contribution "moves the needle" in terms of reaching a lofty goal.

For example, let's say you work as a baggage handler for JetBlue. The corporate mission statement is, "To inspire humanity—both in the air and on the ground." That's a noble ideal, but if you're loading baggage onto an Airbus 220 on the tarmac in Buffalo, New York, at dawn, and it's zero degrees outside and the snow is whipping your face, you might lose sight of the talk about inspiring humanity.

This is why it's a good idea to create mission statements for individual departments or even teams. While it may be difficult for an individual employee to see how his or her contribution fits into the big picture, it's both possible and necessary for the individual employee to know and appreciate how their contribution helps meet the goals of the team.

A basic template for a departmental or team mission statement might include five key elements: "In support of the organization's mission to (_____ the broader organization mission), the mission of (_____ department name) is to (_____ the primary purpose) by providing (_____ primary functions or activities) to (_____ your stakeholders)."

For example, let's say you're the manager of the airport ground crew for an airline company. While it's the mission of the airline to transport people safely from one airport to another, your team's job has little to do with the passengers; you're involved with the *planes*. Using the template above, the mission of your ground crew might be stated as, "In support of Sky Airline's mission to provide low-cost airline service that moves people quickly and safely, the Sky Airlines Ground Crew seeks to ensure the safe and efficient turnaround of aircraft, so they may do the job of transporting our valued passengers, and their personal luggage, to their destinations."

This statement provides both the specific job of the ground crew as well as a link to the bigger picture.

Here's an example. The University of Chicago is a big institution with nearly 20,000 employees in many departments. The Facilities Department is charged with maintaining the physical infrastructure. It even has its own website, where you'll find its mission statement:

> The University of Chicago is a world-class institution of higher education. Its mission is to produce a caliber of teaching and research that regularly leads to advances in fields such as medicine, biology, physics, economics, critical theory, and public policy. Our Facilities Services team supports that mission through efforts to maintain and enhance the University campus and environment and provide superior client service to our community including faculty, students, staff, neighbors, and visitors.[4]

In addition, the Facilities Department has its own vision and core values, as well as a strategic plan.

The department is further divided into four "key units":

1. Capital Project Delivery
2. Facilities Operations
3. Finance and Business Services
4. Campus Planning + Sustainability

Each unit consists of subgroups. For example, within Capital Project Delivery you'll find Landscape Design, Furniture Purchasing, Relocation Management Services, and so on.

This is typical of any large organization. It's common knowledge that an effective project team should be no more than 20 people; if more are involved, they should be split up into two teams. It's fair to say that the mission of a team should be exactly the same for every member of that team, and every member of the team should be personally committed to its success. This requires a uniform level of happiness among all the members. In a large company, happiness is built from the ground up, one level at a time. It goes like this:

- The individual worker is happy to perform his or her tasks and contribute to the success of the team. The work interests them, and they see the value in it for themselves and for other people. The value created may accrue directly to the customer (if the worker happens to be in sales) or to other members of the team or the organization writ large.
- The team consists of happy individuals working together for a common goal, which may be short term ("Let's get that order fulfilled, and then go to the next one!") or long term ("We're pouring the foundation for the new building today.").
- The team may be one of many within a unit, which has its own set of goals.
- Units form a department or division.
- The divisions form the company. The company is directed by the CEO, the board, and the leadership team. They are responsible for the organizational culture, and for ensuring that every employee and stakeholder shares in it and feels good about it.

Take Action!

- ✓ In order to have happy employees, you should have "happy jobs." But there's no "one-size-fits-all" job. There are jobs that some people hate to do, which others find very enjoyable. Be sure you match the employee with the job for which they have a true affinity.
- ✓ Maslow's Hierarchy of Needs is a useful concept to keep in mind. A happy job provides two levels of needs: The basic needs (pay and benefits, schedules, career path, and security and safety) and the higher needs (meaningfulness, personal growth, belonging, achievement, and recognition).
- ✓ Your organization's mission statement is an action-based declaration of the purpose of the organization and how

you serve your customers. Many organizations also have a vision statement, which describes the world the organization is trying to create or is striving for, as well as a statement of values. Ensure these have substantive meaning and your job structure is in alignment with them.

✓ In a big company, create mission statements for individual departments or even teams.

CHAPTER 8

The Happy Company

Sixty years ago, during the vast postwar expansion of the American economy, any company in any industry was considered a "good" company. That is to say, the morality and ethics of businesses were not an issue. If you were a new college graduate in 1960, you didn't think about American corporations in terms of their "goodness" for society. If you were offered a job at Exxon Mobil, Anaconda, American Cyanamid, DuPont Chemicals, Dow Chemical, or Monsanto—all among the Fortune 100— you were happy to accept it. These companies were powerhouses that offered job security and salaries that allowed you to buy a nice house in the suburbs, one or two new cars from Detroit's Big Three automakers, a color TV, and maybe a vacation cabin on the lake. What was good for business was good for America, even as industrial smog enveloped America's cities and the Cuyahoga River in Cleveland actually caught fire because of the volatile pollutants on its surface.

The world has changed since then. Our economy has matured. The brash proclamation made by Milton Friedman in 1970—that a company's sole purpose is to maximize profits for its shareholders, and nothing else matters—has become widely derided, and not just by wild-eyed leftists. True believers in free market capitalism are increasingly of the mind that two things about a company also matter: *what* the company produces and *how* it's produced, in terms of its effect on the community in which it operates and the market it serves.

These days, the best and brightest employees are likely to be discerning about the products of their efforts and will seek out companies that are "socially responsible." Corporate social responsibility (CSR) is a self-defined business model that implies a company is conscious of the impact they have on all aspects of society, including economic, social, and environmental. To embrace CSR means that, in the ordinary course of business, a company is operating in ways that enhance society and the environment, instead of contributing negatively to them. By doing so, the company is focused not just on short-term profits in a way that Milton Friedman might applaud, but on long-term sustainability that does two things: It captures the growing market share of socially responsible consumers and positions the company for long-term growth.

The mission and culture of a company matter to its employees, and if an organization wants to have an engaged workforce they must believe in the mission, integrity, and responsibility of the organization they work for. The happiest employees deeply believe in the organization's core mission, and they also believe in the overarching commitment their organization has in serving others beyond the scope of their business. Obviously, we all want to work for a company that delivers great products, services, and customer experiences. Equally important, however, is the need for an organization to do good things for "goodness sake," that goes far beyond a publicity stunt or some other commercial motive.

Benefit Corporation

Recognized by a majority of state governments and the District of Columbia, a benefit corporation (or in several jurisdictions including Delaware, a public-benefit corporation or PBC) is a for-profit corporate entity that, in addition to profit, includes in its legally defined goals a positive impact on society, workers, the community, and the environment.

What's in the "best interest of the corporation" is specified to include those impacts. In traditional C corporations, those impacts are not specified and directors have no legal obligation to consider them. A benefit corporation's directors and officers operate the business with the same authority and behavior as in a traditional corporation but are required to consider the impact of their decisions not only on shareholders but also on employees, customers, the community, and the local and global environment. Because they are required to consider these impacts, directors are therefore immunized against lawsuits brought by shareholders who, from a Friedman-esque point of view, might accuse them of wasting company money on initiatives that do not produce an obvious and immediate profit.

Typically, a benefit corporation will publish annual benefit report in accordance with recognized third-party standards for defining, reporting, and assessing social and environmental performance.

Investors are increasingly focused on benefit corporations. For example, a survey by Arabesque Partners of 200 academic studies found that "88 percent of reviewed sources find that companies with robust sustainability practices demonstrate better operational performance, which ultimately translates into cash flows," and "80 percent of the reviewed studies demonstrate that prudent sustainability practices have a positive influence on investment performance."[1]

In 2012, the outdoor clothing company Patagonia became the first company in the state of California to register as a benefit corporation. Yvon Chouinard, the founder, wrote, "Benefit corporation legislation creates the legal framework to enable companies like Patagonia to stay mission-driven through succession, capital raises, and even changes in ownership, by institutionalizing the values, culture, processes, and high standards put in place by founding entrepreneurs."[2]

Do the best candidates look for benefit corporations when job hunting? Perhaps not explicitly, but many are aware of the general "vibe" or public image of the company. And they certainly check websites like Glassdoor. There, in December 2021, Patagonia had a robust overall score of 4.3, with 89 percent approval of the CEO, Rose Marcario. If you were a college grad looking for a job in the outdoor apparel industry, you'd definitely check out Patagonia. Here is a typical *negative* review comment: "Culture is welcoming on the surface but you soon find out it is centred around shared interests (surfing, meditation, running, skiing, etc.), and if you don't partake you miss out on a lot of work-related conversations."[3]

Is that as bad as it gets? Then sign me up!

Because benefit corporations are registered on a state-by-state basis, it's difficult to compile a list of the biggest or most prominent ones. Precisely because it's a "low-profile" legal status, many benefit corporations take the next step and become certified B Corporations or B Corps.

The Certified B Corporation

Certified B Corporation is a designation granted by a private nonprofit company, B Lab. Founded in 2006 in Berwyn, Pennsylvania, B Lab created and awards the B corporation certification for for-profit organizations. The "B" stands for "beneficial" and signifies the certified organization voluntarily meets the B Lab standards of transparency, accountability, sustainability, and performance, and intends to create value for society as a whole, not just for its shareholders.

Companies seeking B Corp certification must apply and demonstrate they meet the standards set by B Lab's Standards Advisory Council (SAC). This is an independent multistakeholder council composed of experts on sustainable business from around the world that are responsible for overseeing the performance standards for B Corp certification, including the B Impact Assessment. It consists of two subcommittees, one focused on the overall certification requirements and standards (the Main SAC), and another focused on specific application of the standards for large companies (the Multinational Company Subcommittee).[4]

The B Impact Assessment evaluates how a company's business model and operations impact its workers, customers, community, and environment. From its charitable giving and employee benefits to its supply chain and input materials, B Corp certification demonstrates the business meets the highest standards of verified performance.

Generally, being a legal benefit corporation in your state is a prerequisite for becoming a B Corp. This is because to be a B Corp, you need to have the legal structure and protection that you get with registering as a benefit corporation. In fact—not to confuse you even more—it was in 2010 that B Lab began lobbying US states to pass benefit corporation legislation, a status that is today the legal parallel to the B corporation designation.

Some very big companies have earned B Corp certification. They include:

- Bancolombia, the third largest bank in Latin America, with assets of over $55 billion.
- Danone S.A., a multinational food-products corporation based in Paris and founded in Barcelona, Spain. 2019 revenues were $25.3 billion.
- Unilever PLC, a British multinational consumer goods company headquartered in London, England, with 2020 revenues of EUR50.72 billion.

Just like Glassdoor ranks companies according to their employee reviews, sites such as ZenBusiness.com rank companies according to their B-Corp results.[5] In July 2021, the top-ranked company was South Mountain Company, Inc., an integrated architecture, engineering, building, and renewable energy firm located on Martha's Vineyard in Massachusetts. It topped the global B Corp ranking with a score of 183/200. With just 35 employees, it's not listed on Glassdoor.

Second place was Dr. Bronner's (177.8/200), the family-owned and run company that has become the top-selling brand of organic and fair trade bodycare products in the United States. Sure enough, on Glassdoor, Dr. Bronner's posted an impressive 4.9 score, with 100 percent in both "recommend to a friend" and "approve of CEO" categories. The company is known for its extensive written messages using lots of exclamation points (!). About its employees, the company says, "Be kind, reward generously, support good and healthy living. Seek and encourage the best in one another. For whatever unites us is greater than whatever divides us! We're a family business and consider all who work with us to be part of our extended family. Every 'family member' in every position within the company has an important role to play and deserves to enjoy the best benefits and compensation programs we can offer."[6]

Roughly a third of the company's profits are dedicated to charitable giving and activist causes annually. As an additional symbol of its commitment to its employees, the company has self-imposed caps on executive pay, with executive salaries not to exceed five times the wage of its lowest paid workers.

In third place on the ZenBusiness ranking came Beneficial State Bank (176/200). With assets of about $1 billion, this Oakland, California–based community development bank functions as a regulated financial institution and provides commercial banking services to underserved small and medium-size businesses, nonprofits, affordable-housing developers, community facilities, as well as families and individuals in the Bay Area. Certified as a B-Corp in September 2013, it balances traditional banking practices with a mission to serve the community, not to profit from them.

Here's the bank's statement of beliefs: "We are a community bank that focuses on economic and environmental sustainability and takes a triple-bottom-line approach. We believe that a healthy environment is necessary for economic prosperity. We also believe that we can be a catalyst for positive change in our communities by providing fair, transparent, and sustainable banking products and services."[7]

On Glassdoor, the bank received a respectable rating of 3.6, with 81 percent approval of CEO Kat Taylor.[8]

The Triple Bottom Line

Note the use of the phrase "triple bottom line." Coined by business writer John Elkington in 1994, the triple bottom line (TBL or 3BL) is an accounting framework with three parts: social, environmental (or ecological), and financial. This can be stated as "people, planet, profit." Some organizations have adopted the TBL framework to evaluate their performance in a broader perspective to create greater business value. The concept of TBL demands that a company's responsibility lies with stakeholders rather than shareholders. In this case, "stakeholders" refers to anyone who is influenced, either directly or indirectly, by the actions of the firm.

~ PEOPLE ⁄
‑ PLANET ‑
⁄ PROFIT ~

This is an actual accounting system, with real numbers. For example, the first bottom line would be the company's profit. Let's say the company in question is XYX Chemicals, and the company reports an annual profit of $100 million. Sounds good, doesn't it?

The second bottom line is people. Let's say that in order to make its $100 million in profit, the company's employees have a high rate of cancer, which costs the community an estimated $50 million a year in medical bills and lost wages.

The third bottom line is planet. Let's say the company's factory pollutes the river, causing $50 million in cleanup costs.

When you add them together using the triple bottom line approach, it turns out that XYZ Chemicals returned *zero* profits. Pending lawsuits may even drive it into bankruptcy.

This happened to Dow Corning Corporation in 1995, when it filed for Chapter 11 bankruptcy because it could not afford both to contribute $2 billion to a breast implant litigation settlement fund and to defend itself against product liability claims outside the settlement. In the first quarter of 1995, Dow Corning had posted record sales and earnings of $611 million and $49.5 million, respectively. The case dragged on, and in

1998 the company agreed to pay $3.2 billion to settle claims from about 170,000 women who said their silicone breast implants made them sick. The company finally emerged from bankruptcy in 2004.

On the other end of the spectrum, let's say ABC Chemicals is a socially responsible B-Corp. The company posts an annual profit of $20 million.

For people, the company's employees experience the same rate of cancer as the community as a whole, so there's no bottom line impact; but the company spends $10 million a year on community literacy and job training programs.

For the planet, the company does not pollute the river, and instead it funds a reforestation program valued at $10 million a year.

Using the triple bottom line approach, you could say that ABC Chemicals returned $40 million in value to its stakeholders, including $20 million in cash to its immediate investors.

The TBL approach has been used to criticize employers who pay many full-time employees less than a living wage, forcing them to supplant their paychecks with government welfare benefits. In 2020, the nonpartisan Government Accountability Office reported that Walmart and McDonald's were among the top employers of beneficiaries of federal aid programs like Medicaid and food stamps. AS CNBC reported, the GAO analyzed data from Medicaid agencies in six states and Supplemental Nutrition Assistance Program (SNAP, or food stamps) agencies in nine states. The agency found that Walmart was the top employer of Medicaid enrollees in three states and one of the top four employers in the remaining three states. The retailer was the top employer of SNAP recipients in five states and one of the top four employers in the remaining four states.

Other big companies with a large number of employees on federal aid included Amazon, Kroger, and Dollar General.

The question was, exactly how profitable are these companies when taxpayers are asked to subsidize the low wages of their employees through social safety net benefits? If you applied TBL accounting to them, you might find that the company's "investors" include not just shareholders but taxpayers who are not benefitting from stock value or dividends.

Take Action!

- ✓ To have happy employees, you need happy jobs. To have happy jobs, you need a happy company. If there are internal conflicts that create misery—if the company is a polluter, or has poor working conditions, or makes an unhealthy product—then it'll be difficult to create a happy company.
- ✓ Be aware that potential employees and investors are increasingly interested in the level of social responsibility of your company. The best, happiest employees want to feel as though their company is one of the "good guys."
- ✓ Think about the triple bottom line approach and its appeal to your stakeholders. Don't assume that your investors care only about the cash profit and not what you're doing for your people and the planet. Don't assume that your employees just want their paychecks and are oblivious to the "big picture" of the company's role in the community. If you ignore these trends, you may face a steady erosion of investor and employee quality. Always aim to be the best and attract the best!

CHAPTER 9

The Happiness Ecosystem

In order for happiness to take root in an organization from top to bottom, it needs to be a systematic process that engages all the players within the delicate ecosystem of the organization. We use the term "ecosystem" because it accurately describes some interesting phenomena that occur within an organization. In nature, an ecosystem comprises the organisms and the physical environment with which they interact. These biotic and abiotic components are linked together through nutrient cycles and energy flows, all powered by energy from the sun in the form of heat and light.

Every entity in an ecosystem depends on every other entity, either directly or indirectly. A change in the temperature of an ecosystem will affect what plants will grow there, for instance. A change in plant life will affect the survival of local animals, and so on.

In a biological ecosystem, the term *symbiosis* refers to a situation where two species have a direct relationship in a way that benefits both. Organisms can depend upon other organisms for cleaning, protection, or gathering food. There are five types of symbiosis; the one that we're interested in is "mutualism," which is a long-lasting, mutually beneficial symbiotic relationship.

In some mutualistic relationships, the organisms can't survive without each other. For example, bees gather nectar from flowers, which they make into food. If there were no flowers, the bees could not survive. As they go from flower to flower, pollen rubs onto their bodies, and the pollen then falls off into the next flower, which pollinates it. Without this bee-assisted pollination, the flowering plant would not survive.

Here's another example, which is very close to home, so to speak. Every human has a strong mutualistic relationship with the trillions of beneficial bacteria living in their digestive tract. This "microbiome"—which can weigh as much as five pounds—is critical for digestion and regulates the intestinal environment. In return, the bacteria get a nice warm place to live and all the food they want. It's a good deal for both parties!

The comparison to the workplace is easy to make.

In any organization of more than one person, success depends upon every participant producing to their maximum capacity *in concert with the others*, toward a common goal. Energy that's directed in a non-essential direction is wasted. Energy directed *against* the common direction is destructive. When people are unhappy at work, they're far more likely to work aimlessly or even against the common direction.

One of the most common forms of sabotage is to undermine a fellow employee who is perceived to stand in the way of a promotion or other form of reward. Such behavior forces the target to waste time and energy by playing defense, by forming alliances, complaining to human resources, or saving evidence in the form of emails and other messages. All of this amounts to more wasted and destructive energy.

Negative behavior is contagious. Researchers at Harvard University found that even the most honest employees become more likely to commit misconduct if they work alongside a dishonest individual. The flow of influence goes from the bad person to the good person—that is, among coworkers, it appears easier to learn bad behavior than good. As Stephen Dimmock and William C. Gerken reported in *Harvard Business Review*, it's important that managers realize the costs of a destructive employee go beyond the direct effects of that employee's actions, as bad behaviors of one employee influence the behaviors of other employees through peer effects. By underestimating these spillover effects, a few malignant employees can infect an otherwise healthy corporate culture.[1]

It takes only one unhappy employee with behavioral issues to become the "bad apple" that inflames negative feelings and attitude within the rest of the team and destroys a mutualistic symbiosis. A bad apple in this case is someone who behaves legally (that is, breaks no law) but is manifestly unhappy and negative. An experiment on team effectiveness and employee misbehavior by Will Felps, Terence R. Mitchell, and Eliza Byington found that having just one rogue employee in a team can reduce the group's performance by up to 40 percent. As they wrote in "How, When, and Why Bad Apples Spoil the Barrel," many people have had the personal experience of working with someone who displayed bad apple behaviors. When this emerges at work, it consumes inordinate amounts of time, psychological resources, and emotional energy. Such behaviors can "offend us, reduce our enthusiasm, change our mood and may ultimately lead us to personally de-identify or leave the group, with a high likelihood that the group itself will perform poorly, fail, or disband."[2]

The goal is to create a workplace ecosystem where there is robust symbiosis among all participants, and the spirit of happiness allows for mutual trust and sublimation of personal ego for the common good.

Examples of symbiosis in the workplace include:

- The feeling of satisfaction and personal worth when helping a coworker achieve satisfaction in their work.
- The feeling of integrity when we make certain that a coworker is acknowledged and given credit for work that both employees completed together.
- The personal satisfaction of making coworkers, managers, and executives feel appreciated and their contribution to the organization that is humanistic.

Note that the focus is on how the participant *feels* about their work. When it comes to many life-altering decisions that humans make, nearly every time, emotion will prevail over logic.

Be Happy with Competition and Change

In a biological ecosystem, many species compete for the finite resources of food. This is what drives the survival of the fittest. Although you can tune into endless nature documentaries to see plenty of animals enjoying happy fun, the law of nature always takes precedence, and among animals, the concept of individual happiness often takes a distant back seat to the realities of survival.

We humans have more choices. In the work/life ecosystem, most of us can leave an ecosystem—a company or an industry—that does not offer sufficient abundance. If we're working at a job and we are not able to have a growth pathway that allows us to compete favorably, we have the ultimate authority to decide to move to a better ecosystem.

The bottom line is, in the workforce ecosystem there is little competition at the top for dedicated, thoughtful, and productive employees. In other words, there is little competition for the truly talented; there is intense competition for the mediocre and the incompetent.

It pays to be happy and highly qualified. In every hierarchical organization such as a corporation, not every employee gets paid the same or has the same perks. In fact, the pay gap between front-line employees and top-level executives is getting wider.

The Economic Policy Institute (EPI) estimates that CEO compensation has grown 1,322 percent since 1978, while typical worker compensation has risen just 18 percent. In 2020, CEOs of the top 350 firms in the United States made $24.2 million, on average—351 times more than a typical worker.[3]

This makes it even more imperative that leaders dedicate themselves to serving their employees and cultivating a genuine culture of happiness within the organization. It also means that every participant in the race must be happy with the reality of life.

The market, our work, and our career paths are the subjects of rapid and amorphous change. Every industry and marketplace are subject to disruption. The nature of this disruption is fast, and for some confusing. Career success requires consistent adaptation, and to do this, you need to be *happy with change.* The best organizations and employees understand that change is occurring at a faster rate than ever and survival depends on adaptive change. In Darwin's work, he points out quite accurately that the species that survive are those able to adapt to environmental and other changes. The best organizations hardwire change into their employee's career pathway in order to make certain that they have the skills and even the philosophy of adaptation. And the most successful individuals embrace change and find happiness within it.

In the Happiness Ecosystem, Everyone's a Customer

Organizations that deliver exceptional *employee* experiences always also deliver exceptional *customer* and *stakeholder* experiences. When I say stakeholders, I mean anyone you engage with in the course of the business day, which includes:

- Investors
- Vendors
- Partners
- Customers
- Regulators
- Community organizations
- Neighboring businesses
- Your board of directors
- Employees

These may seem to be independent groups with their own interests, which in many ways they are. But how you *treat* them is really the same across the board: You treat them as if each and every one was a customer, and your job is to please them and ensure they'll stay loyal to you and your brand. This becomes easy to conceptualize if you remember that a customer is someone with whom you make an exchange of value. In the old days, this could have been bartering. If you owned a blacksmith shop, your customer may have paid for his new horseshoes with a sack of flour. While today's customers use money, the idea is the same: You provide something of value to them, and they reciprocate.

It goes without saying that a happy, friendly salesperson will sell more than a rude, surly one. This is "Sales 101." But how about all the other exchanges of value we make every day? Would not the same rule apply?

For example, your board of directors provides wise guidance (a thing of value), and in exchange they receive the benefits of networking and the prestige of serving on your board. If you, the CEO, are trying to manage your board, it's a thousand times easier if you treat them the way you would treat a customer—put a smile on your face and at least *act* happy.

Your employees provide a service to you and your company, and in return you pay them money and other forms of compensation. In effect, you are each other's customers. You agree to an exchange of value that benefits both parties. Especially in today's competitive job market, doesn't it make sense to work from a position of happiness?

If you treat these various constituencies the way you treat your valued customers, it does not mean that you "roll over" for them or surrender your rights. If a customer said, "I like this widget you're selling, and I want you to give it to me for free," you'd smile and reply, "I'm sorry, that's not possible. May I interest you in our thrifty payment plan?" Contrary to the popular saying, just because someone is a customer does not make them always right.

Please note that not everyone is your *literal* customer. There are many people with whom you may never have an exchange of value, particularly if you operate in the B2B space, where a company's customer base is typically very narrow and well defined. Any good marketing expert will tell you to avoid wasting time and resources trying to sell to someone who will never be your customer. When we say you should treat everyone like a customer, we mean the people who are already in your universe or who are likely to enter.

How you define "customer" becomes your manifestation of your vision and your professional expertise, and your pathway to creating value for your organization. It's how you move from being perceived as an order-taker to serving your customers as an innovator and leader.

Sometimes people separate customers and stakeholders into four subcategories:

1. Internal customers are your process partners. They are usually in the same company or line of business as you, but are your downstream processes or department.
2. External customers are the people and clients who purchase your company's products or services.
3. Internal stakeholders include your employees, the management and leadership team, and the owners of the business.
4. External stakeholders include the government, regulators, investors and shareholders, and suppliers and vendors.

This is fine, but it doesn't change the fact of how you behave with them and treat them. Highly effective people know that happiness elicits and fosters more happiness in others, and like ripples in a pond, keep radiating outward.

Using the RealRatings System

If you're a small business owner with a handful of employees, it's easy to know their individual levels of happiness. You probably have personal contact with them on a daily basis, and if someone seems unhappy, you'll know. But in a large organization, the CEO simply cannot personally interact with all the employees; and if interaction occurs, especially with employees who are either low-level or who have some reason to want to flatter the boss, the employee is likely to put on a happy face so the leader will think everything's fine.

This is where the RealRatings system is particularly useful. The RealRatings surveys can help you uncover two different but related data sets:

1. Things your employees think could be improved in the company. They may reveal they hate the phone system, or how the customer management databases are set up, or the vacation scheduling policy with human resources. An employee could be personally happy and still offer criticisms of his or her job conditions.

2. How your employees feel about themselves and their tenures at the company. In a perfect world, everyone would come to work with a positive attitude and leave their personal troubles at the door. But that doesn't always happen. Even though an employee may strive to *act* happy, personal problems can spill over into our professional life too. Financial, health, or relationship worries can make it challenging for an employee to focus on their job and remain enthusiastic and diligent.

Because the RealRatings questionnaire specifically asks the employee what they hate about their job, and gives them permission to vent their feelings, it's very useful for taking the pulse of overall employee happiness.

A Happy Company: Adobe

Happiness is a subjective state of mind that manifests itself through measurable outcomes. You may not know for certain if someone is truly happy, but you can get a good idea by looking at what they do and say. So what does a happy company look like? Can you tell from the outside that Company A has happier employees than Company B?

In 2021, Comparably, a workplace culture and corporate brand reputation platform, released the results of their survey of the top 50 large companies and top 50 small/medium companies (500 employees or fewer). They amassed over 15 million anonymous ratings from employees at over 70,000 companies. The company that came out on top was Adobe, the American multinational computer software company. Headquartered in San Jose, California, it has historically specialized in software for the creation and publication of a wide range of content, including graphics, photography, illustration, animation, multimedia/video, motion pictures and print.

The Comparably survey questions include a few that asked for written comments by the 893 Adobe employees who responded. Here are a few samples, with their original spelling and punctuation:

- "Overall I feel that I am doing work that matters, and I am being recognised for it. I fell I am learning everyday and I am seeing the career progression."
- "We are a team, we are relatively knew and very supportive of each other, and fun."
- "It's an all inclusive company and the first one I have worked at that actual cares about diversity and is focused on driving positive change."

To its credit, the survey asked for negative opinions (this is a rarity!). One question was, "What do your coworkers need to improve and how could you work together better?"

A response from an employee in the product department was, "There is a lack of caring at Workfront. Everyone deflects ownership of duties whenever possible. When they do get assigned ownership, they do the bare minimum. There is no pride and it's contagious."

There's an unhappy employee! And here's one from the engineering department:

Managers should stop boasting about how many hours they work in a day and how they work on weekends. Everyone likes to work more once in a while but it's stressful to have someone constantly berating you for not doing it on a daily basis. People can have personal commitments.[4]

It's difficult to tell where these unhappy employees work because Adobe is a global company with 24,500 employees in 68 office locations across 26 countries.

Other global legacy companies that made the top 10 list include Microsoft (5), Farmers Insurance (6), IBM (7), and Experian (10).

Under the leadership of chairman, president, and CEO Shantanu Narayen, Adobe strives to put the happiness of its employees front and center. As the company says:

So, what exactly is behind our award-winning company culture? It's simple: Since its inception in 1982, Adobe has always taken a people-based approach to business, fostering a diverse and inclusive workplace environment that is committed to making employees feel happy, appreciated, comfortable and excited to bring their best selves to work.[5]

Adobe also made it on the *Forbes* "America's Best Employers" list for 2020, ranked at #27. At the top spot was the University of Alabama at Birmingham Hospital, where many of its 23,000 employees were caring for thousands of pandemic-stricken patients while educating America's future doctors and nurses. Also making the top 10 was one of my personal favorites, In-N-Out Burger, based in Irvine, California. This fast-food chain has 358 locations and about 8,000 very happy employees.[6]

For the sixth year in a row, in 2021 Adobe made *Fortune Magazine's* list of "25 World's Best Workplaces," ranking #21. The global designation was awarded because the company was recognized as a Best Workplace in Australia, France, Germany, India, Ireland, Japan, the United Kingdom and the United States. The one area where the company seemed to have scored hate points was in compensation; only 79 percent of employees agreed with the statement, "I feel I receive a fair share of the profits made by this organization."[7]

At the top of the *Fortune* list was DHL Express, headquartered in Bonn, Germany, with 111,000 global employees.

While there are many such "best company" lists and many differences between them, if you look at them you tend to see the same names. Indeed, Adobe showed up at #16 on *People* magazine's "100 Companies That Care 2021" list. The announcement highlighted the company's philanthropic efforts. The company committed $1 million to match—and then double—employee donations made to groups addressing the Covid-19 pandemic, with more than $1.6 million ultimately raised. In addition, the company committed $4.6 million to organizations providing assistance locally and across the world.

"The people at Adobe genuinely care about each other and their communities," said an employee. "It shows in the volunteering activities that employees sponsor at work and in their personal lives."[8]

Take Action!

- ✓ An ecosystem comprises the organisms and the physical environment in which and with which they interact. Your organization is an ecosystem, and its success depends upon every participant producing to their maximum capacity in concert with the others, toward a common goal.
- ✓ Within your ecosystem, negative behavior—promulgated by unhappy employees—is contagious. The costs of just one destructive employee go beyond the direct effects of that employee's actions, as their bad behavior can influence the behavior of other employees through peer effects.
- ✓ Symbiosis at work is a mutually beneficial relationship between different employees or teams. The goal is to create a workplace ecosystem where there is robust symbiosis among all participants, and the spirit of happiness allows for mutual trust and sublimation of personal ego for the common good.
- ✓ Career success requires consistent adaptation, and to do this, your employees need to be happy with change.
- ✓ Treat every stakeholder—employee, investor, vendor, board member—as if each and every one was a customer, and your job is to please them and ensure they'll stay loyal to you and your brand.
- ✓ The RealRatings surveys can help you uncover two different but related data sets:
  1. Things your employees think could be improved in the company.
  2. How your employees feel about themselves and their tenures at the company.

CHAPTER 10

Human Experience Design

The widely used term "customer experience" (CX) describes the way in which organizations architect positive experiences across their customer's journey. It's a powerful concept, and big organizations spend hundreds of millions of dollars with the goal of getting deeper insights and delivering better experiences to their customers. In return for this investment, they hope to experience organizational growth, more sales, and of course higher profits.

This area is both complex and fascinating, and in fact I've written two books on the subject, including *What Customers Crave* and *What Customers Hate*, both published by HarperCollins Leadership.

The problem with typical customer experience strategies is that they are fractional—in other words, not complete. The core challenge is that an organization cannot deliver exceptional *customer* experiences without first and foremost delivering exceptional *employee* experiences across the journey of every employee. One must come from the other. Consequently, organizations need to value the employee experience just as much as they do the customer experience.

This introduces the principle of an overall *human* experience (HX) design and the creation of a formal strategy called (not surprisingly)

Happiness as a Strategy (HaaS). I'll dive much more deeply into HaaS in the chapters ahead.

CX is dependent upon employee experience. Only happy employees are capable of delivering exceptional customer experiences that help organizations drive brand value and enterprise growth.

Meanwhile, the reverse is true as well: Employee experience is influenced by customer experience. Unhappy customers can make work life miserable for employees as they attempt to appease their legitimate concerns. It's a symbiotic circle that goes 'round and 'round.

HX design focuses on the people who power a business to success, providing them with the tools and technology to enable productive, meaningful, and personal employee experiences that drive business results.

Why has this concept rocketed to prominence? Part of the answer lies with the pace of innovation that we've been experiencing since the dawn of the digital revolution. But a bigger factor is the massive upheaval to the workplace that began in early 2020 when the Covid-19 pandemic swept across the globe. It was almost exactly a century after the last great pandemic—the Spanish flu—had killed up on to 50 million people worldwide, and we humans were caught off-guard. As we all celebrated the New Year, the last thing most people were worried about was a global viral pandemic that would shatter their lives for the next two years and beyond.

The Mixed Blessings of More Remote Work

The Covid-19 pandemic massively disrupted the workplaces of companies large and small. The short-term consequences were sudden and severe: Millions of people were furloughed or lost their jobs, and millions more adjusted to working from home as offices closed. Not surprisingly, during the pandemic the virus and the resulting shutdowns most severely disturbed industries with the highest level of customer-employee physical proximity: medical care, personal care, on-site customer service (restaurants, banks, gyms, retail stores), and leisure and travel.

As the pandemic brought many customer-service businesses to a screeching halt, the effects of quarantine, isolation, and travel restriction strategies had a brutal impact on the economy and many industries, with the financial markets punishing investors with steep declines. The 2020 stock market crash was a major and sudden global stock market crash that began on February 20, 2020, and ended on April 7, though US market indices did not return to January 2020 levels until November 2020.

The pandemic collided with the accelerating pace of innovation, creating a two-pronged disruption that left many workers wondering, "How will I stay relevant, hold onto my job, or find one in the future?" Many workers took matters into their own hands. According to the "Workforce Evolution Study" conducted by HP, rather than waiting for support from their employers, nearly one in three employees took it into their own hands to reskill and make significant investments in home office supplies and technologies, with some realizing they could find more success as entrepreneurs. Nearly half of the surveyed employees spent their own money on technology upgrades such as security software, new laptops, and home printers.[1]

Meanwhile, as if to confirm the fears of employees, in the Covid-19 economy employers are embracing increased automation. According to a 2020 survey of executives, 73 percent of respondents said their organizations had embarked on a path to intelligent automation, representing a significant 58 percent jump from the number reported in 2019. Many of the businesses surveyed said the pandemic had caused their organizations to reexamine how work was done, with a majority already implementing robotic process automation and many more planning on it.[2]

If you consider only remote work that can be done without a loss of productivity, it's estimated that up to 25 percent of the workforces in Asian and Western industrialized nations could successfully do their jobs from home between three and five days a week. This represents as much as five times more remote work than before the pandemic and could trigger a seismic shift in the geography of work, as individuals and companies migrate further away from large cities into suburbs and rural areas.

Especially as populations in Asian and Western nations flatline or even decline over the next few decades, this shift will lead to a drop in demand for office space, restaurants, and retail stores in downtown areas, and for public transportation. Remote work may also impact business travel, as the exploding use of videoconferencing during the pandemic has fostered an increased acceptance of videoconferencing.

(Meanwhile, in emerging economies, particularly African nations with rapidly growing populations, cities are expected to become even bigger. By 2100, the three biggest cities in the world are projected to be Lagos, Nigeria; Kinshasa, Democratic Republic of Congo; and Dar Es Salaam, United Republic of Tanzania, with a combined population of about 245 million people.)[3]

Consumers, too, embraced the convenience of e-commerce and other online activities during the pandemic. In 2020, the share of e-commerce grew at two to five times the previous rate.

The biggest retailers in the United States including Amazon, Walmart, and Target received the lion's share of the e-commerce tsunami. According to a study by Digital Commerce 360, reported on Inc., the top 500 companies generated $849.5 billion in online sales in 2020, a 45.3 percent increase year-over-year and the biggest jump since Digital Commerce 360 began tracking the statistic in 2006. Much of that windfall went to the big guys, because during the pandemic the large companies that were considered "essential" retail reaped huge profits thanks to brand loyalty, the breadth of their offerings, and the ability to easily return items.[4]

In 2020, the first year of the pandemic, Amazon reported a net income of $21.33 billion, nearly double its $11.6 billion net income in the previous year. During the same fiscal period, the company's revenue amounted to more than $386 billion.[5]

The question becomes, as work becomes increasingly remote, and you're not physically seeing many of your employees on a daily basis, how do you know they're happy?

The good news—at least for companies with remote workers—is that a study by Owl Labs found that full-time remote workers reported being happy in their jobs 22 percent more than workers who were never remote. In the "State of Remote Work 2019"—before the pandemic—remote workers reported having better work-life balance, focus, and less stress. Companies that gave workers more flexibility were more likely to retain them. Remote workers would also work longer hours; they reported working over 40 hours per week 43 percent more than nonremote workers. Remote work is increasingly popular with senior executives, who said they worked remotely at least once per week 34 percent more than those in lower positions. (Being a top exec has its perks!)[6]

But a word of warning: The movement toward increased remote work is very new. Its long-term effects are unknown. And many of the tensions that affect project teams in physical offices—rivalries, suspicions, employees resenting a slacker—aren't going to disappear when workers are communicating over videoconference calls.

Remote Work, Same Hate Points

Research has shown that remote work can produce the same negative hate points as in-person work.

A survey of over 4,000 UK office workers by Microsoft and YouGov found that more than half (56 percent) felt they were generally happier when they were able to work from home. But this positive attitude toward remote working did not necessarily translate to the work itself.

Nearly one in three (30 percent) of those surveyed said they were working more hours while working from home, with over half saying they felt they had to be available at all times (53 percent) as well as take fewer breaks (52 percent).

As reported in "Work Smarter to Live Better," Microsoft said the findings suggested a disconnect between staff expectations and employer demands, suggesting that staff felt they owed their bosses longer hours in return for being able to work from home.

"The positive impact on happiness caused by being based at home comes at the cost of visibility—meaning staff feel they need to show their worth by putting in a longer shift," the report said.

At the same time, more employees are seeking out mental health resources as a result of these renewed pressures, and employers are falling short.

Microsoft found that 36 percent of employees sought mental health and resilience resources, yet only 29 percent of organizations had introduced additional benefits and resources to support employees' physical and mental well-being.

Ironically, the survey revealed that employees working in industries most severely impacted by the pandemic received the least support. Finance, accounting, IT, and telecom industries provided generous support, according to their employees, while employees in medical and health services felt poorly supported.[7]

A lack of real human interaction has become a problem. Atif Hafeez, a CFO in the private equity sector, said in TechRepublic, "Unlike the pre-Covid working environment, we don't have the luxury of in-person meetings when our teams are working from home. Therefore, we are training our team managers as to how to be more effective under the given circumstances.

"Previously the external counsel was enlisted only when it was specifically needed. Now, we are having to retain the external counsel to support our staff because the need for that is rather regular."[8]

Working from home has made many employees feel isolated and overworked.

A survey of 2,000 Americans by OnePoll on behalf of Front, a company that offers collaborative email for customer communication, revealed that staying in your pajamas and working from home every day isn't all sweetness and light. Sixty-three percent of respondents said they felt like the hate points outweighed the love points, so much so that 3 in 10 people said they had considered quitting their job since beginning the pandemic-mandated remote work. The same number of people said they even considered changing careers altogether.

As reported in the *Miami Herald*, the survey showed the top three reasons why people considered quitting were unreasonable workloads in short periods of time (17 percent), lack of connection to their team (14 percent), and their company's poor handling of their transition from in-person to remote locations (14 percent).

And here's an unexpected hate point: Without traffic to beat or a train to catch, many people who found themselves working from home said they felt like their workdays had gotten longer. Fully one-half of respondents said they spent five or more additional hours working remotely each week.[9]

The fact is that remote work presents technological challenges that may not be fully resolved. Consider your average team meeting at a traditional workplace. Everyone goes into the conference room, sits around the table, and talks. This is the way humans have been conducting meetings for thousands of years. When the ancient Egyptians built the Great Pyramid of Giza, the project managers probably sat at a table and worked out their plans. It was—and still is—face-to-face and low-tech. No fancy equipment needed.

Suddenly, the technology took center stage. The OnePoll survey found that at-home offices created hate points from communication being done over too many digital platforms (41 percent), a "significant uptick" in online messages with coworkers (34 percent), insufficient IT support (34 percent), and general confusion due to spotty communication between different teams across a company (32 percent). "More apps create more noise—and noise is stressful in an already challenging year," said Nate Abbott, head of product at Front, in a news release sent to McClatchy News. "Particularly with a remote workforce, teammates need to be able to collaborate and lean on each other, while being closer to their customers. There's really no better opportunity to witness the impact of your work than when you can see the effect of your work on a customer's life."[10]

Employee anxiety is exacerbated by the fact that—for whatever reason—employers either don't know or aren't sharing their plans for their Covid-19 economy working arrangements. While some organizations may have revealed their general intent to embrace extended virtual work going forward, too few of them have shared detailed policies, guidelines, expectations, and approaches. This lack of life-altering specifics is leaving many employees anxious.

To create a true human experience that allows all stakeholders to set aside their anxieties about the shape of the Covid-19 economy, leaders need to communicate frequently with their employees, even if their plans have yet to fully solidify. Organizations that articulate clear and specific policies and approaches for the future workplace will see employee productivity and well-being rise.

Every organization should make HX design a priority as soon as possible. This is because organizations are generally good at carefully planning facilities, capital, marketing, advertising placement, and everything else. What they *don't* tend to do very well is to create an integrated strategy that ensures that they're serving everyone within their vested ecosystem. I refer to this as a "vested" ecosystem because it includes everyone within the touch of a given organization. Organizations that improve the quality of experiences for their employees, partners, customers, vendors, and all that they serve are far more profitable and enjoy the benefits of sustainable growth and brand value.

The Most Miserable Companies

In the previous chapter we looked at a selection of companies that scored high on lists of happy places to work, with a focus on Adobe, although there are many other worthy contenders. This exercise reminds us of the famous first sentence of Leo Tolstoy's novel *Anna Karenina*: "Happy families are all alike; every unhappy family is unhappy in its own way." In one sense, this is true. If you read about happy companies, they all share certain characteristics, and chief among them is a CEO who is committed to a happy company culture and happy employees.

How about the opposite? Is Tolstoy correct? Are miserable companies each unhappy in their own way?

Perhaps they are. When you read about horrible companies you see many repeated patterns, all centering around greed and indifference. But there's one important element that ties them all together.

I'll put it plainly: If the CEO is a jerk, then the company will be a place of misery.

There may be other contributing factors, but with the CEO the buck stops and the attitude starts. The CEO sets the tone, which is emulated by all the executives who wish to please him or her, and on down to the last guy on the loading dock at midnight.

But we'll dive into the role of the CEO in more detail in the pages ahead. For now, let's take the measure of some companies that—fairly or unfairly—have acquired the reputation for miserable employees.

In December 2020, Yahoo published its list of "The 17 Worst Companies to Work for in America." Their list reflected the worst-rated companies on Glassdoor, focusing on those with at least 10,000 employees and 1,000 reviews. In the case of ties, they prioritized companies based on one metric: if workers would be *least likely* to recommend the company to a friend.[11]

Yahoo noted that each of these despised businesses had its own special problems. Some employees cited poor management or a toxic company culture, while others pointed to high staff turnover and abysmally low pay. But you can guess the ultimate source of all these problems!

Interestingly, three of the top five worst employers were legacy railroad companies: Union Pacific Railroad (1), Norfolk Southern Railroad (2), and CSX (5).

At the top of the list was Union Pacific Railroad. Founded in 1862, in 2020 this freight-hauling railroad had 31,000 employees and operated 7,600 locomotives over 32,313 miles of routes in 23 US states west of the Mississippi River.[12]

Why the mountain of hate points? On Glassdoor, the company received less than two stars. Only 12 percent of employees would recommend it to a friend, and only half that number—6 percent—approved of CEO Lance Fritz.

Railroad work is tough, and a work-life imbalance is common at rail companies, but many employees cited a lack of job security. During the onset of the Covid-19 pandemic, citing the unexpected drop in freight volume, CEO Fritz announced four months of furloughs. He also said that executives would take a 25 percent pay cut during that time as well, but workers weren't impressed, and gave senior management the lowest of the company's extremely low scores.

If you read the online chat rooms featuring UP employees, the people expressing their opinions tend to fall into three distinct camps:

1. Union Pacific is a hotbed of racism, blatant favoritism, and corporate greed and indifference.
2. Union Pacific is a workplace of tremendous diversity where you'll find managers of every race and color.
3. Railroad workers love to complain—all the way to the bank! Locomotive engineers, train dispatchers, and many others earn over $100,000 a year. They proclaim their misery while cashing their generous paychecks.

On Indeed.com, the company earned an average of 2.8 stars out of 5. Compensation/benefits was the highest rated at 3.8 stars. Meanwhile, work/life balance and management each received just 2.3 stars.

A very insightful comment was posted in November 2021 by a former locomotive conductor. This person wrote, "There is money to be made working for the Union Pacific Railroad, but it is blood money. The work-life balance is rough but expected. They warn you about the long hours, remaining on call in order to make your full wage, and working nights, weekends, and holidays, and how it makes strains family life. That is understandable for a healthy wage and benefits, but the company has definitely done everything possible to make it feel as if it's not worth it at all. . . . Union Pacific corporate management is doing everything they can to remove freedoms, perks, and even everything fair about this career."

Offering the minority viewpoint was this director of signal and telecommunication maintenance, who gave the company 5 stars: "Great place to work just difficult due to travel for work purposes. . . . Enjoyed my time at Union Pacific. Unfortunately could not get back home so being away from home was difficult for my life/work balance."

One more, from a diesel electrician: "Company hates you. Management just trying to survive."[13]

Everyone can agree that railroading is a tough job, with many positions offering good pay but hard physical work, extensive travel, long hours, and missed family time. But for people who accept those conditions—and there are many—why should they hate the company so much?

The same problems appear at Norfolk Southern, which ranked #2 on the Yahoo list. On Indeed.com, we saw the same employee complaints as for Union Pacific. The worst ratings were for work-life balance and management, followed by culture and job security/advancement. The highest rating was for compensation/benefits. The employees were well paid—and they still hated the company. This locomotive electrician wrote, "Workers typically get along well, but the company as a whole is purely profit driven. I felt as though the company didn't put any value in me being part of the team. This feeling was discussed and agreed upon by all co-workers. I was told on multiple occasions, 'Just be thankful you have a job.' Morale was basically non-existent."[14]

On Glassdoor, Norfolk Southern earned a dismal 2.2 stars. Only 17 percent would recommend to a friend, and the same low percentage approved of CEO James A. Squires.[15]

The question is, can you operate a railroad company—admittedly the work is tough—without your employees hating you?

To find out, all you have to do is Google "best railroad company to work for."

We did, and found a website called Train Conductor HQ. They rated the BNSF Railway Company as the best railroad to work for. BNSF—the name is derived from the 1996 merger of the Burlington Northern and the

Santa Fe Railway—is the largest freight railroad network in North America, with 41,000 employees, 32,500 miles of track in 28 states, and more than 8,000 locomotives. In 2019, BNSF reported $23.515 billion in revenue.

And by the way, in 2010 the railroad's parent company became a wholly owned subsidiary of Berkshire Hathaway, Inc., whose chairman and CEO is Warren Buffett.

On Glassdoor, BNSF earned a respectable 3.1 stars. Thirty-nine percent would recommend it to a friend, while 42 percent approved of president and CEO Kathryn Farmer.[16]

Yes, the head of the largest and most profitable railroad in the United States is a woman.

After graduating from Texas Christian University with a bachelor of business administration and an MBA in finance, she joined Burlington Northern Railroad in 1992 as a management trainee. Through various mergers, she has spent her entire career with the company, holding positions in operations, marketing, and finance. In September 2018 Farmer was made BNSF executive vice president operations. On January 1, 2021, she succeeded Carl Ice as president and CEO, and was also made chair of BNSF's board of directors.

On Glassdoor, the reviews are similar in substance to those you'll see directed at Union Pacific and Norfolk Southern—good pay and benefits, but long hours, difficult work conditions, and gripes about management. To be honest, the three companies all do the same thing. They're very similar in their daily operations. The big difference is in the *degree* of hate and love. You can see that while some employees really hate BNSF and give it one star, they are far fewer in number than the employees of Union Pacific and Norfolk Southern who hate their jobs, while the number of employees who generally love BNSF is greater. Across an organization with 41,000 employees, this *reduction of hate points* and *increase in love points* can make a huge difference in the company's overall performance.

On Indeed.com, BNSF had an overall rating of 3.4 stars. At the top was pay and benefits with 4.1 stars, while at the bottom was work-life balance at 2.6 stars and management at 2.7 stars. These were similar numbers to Union Pacific and Norfolk Southern—a bit better, but not dramatically so.

The biggest difference was how the employees felt about their CEO. They may have recognized that no one person could change the fundamental nature of railroad work—long hours, time away from home—but the CEO could do a lot to help the employees feel a sense of pride, self-worth, and—yes—happiness.

If you're the CEO, what does this matter to you? It should matter a lot. If you want your company to be profitable, you must recruit the best employees. You want happy people who relish coming to work each morning. Now pretend you're a bright young college graduate with a *summa cum laude* degree in engineering, and you want to work at a railroad. You do your research. You read about Union Pacific and BNSF and all the others. Because these companies all do the same thing, on what will you base your decision to apply? You'll apply to the company with the most positive culture, where the employees seem happiest, and where your work will be appreciated. Who would want to work at a company where everyone seems miserable? The answer is simple: the people who can't get a job anywhere else.

You want the very best for your company. That's why you must embrace the Happy Work Principle and make your company the first choice of the best and the brightest.

Take Action!

- ✓ Your organization cannot deliver exceptional customer experiences without first and foremost delivering exceptional employee experiences across the journey of every employee. One must come from the other. Only happy employees are capable of delivering exceptional customer experiences that help organizations drive brand value and enterprise growth.
- ✓ The reverse is true as well: Employee experience is influenced by customer experience. Unhappy customers can make work life miserable for employees as they

attempt to appease their legitimate concerns. It's a symbiotic circle that goes 'round and 'round. This is why your focus must be on human experience (HX) design.

✓ HE design focuses on the people who power a business to success, providing them with the tools and technology to enable productive, meaningful, and personal employee experiences that drive business results.

✓ In the Covid-19 economy, remote work is surging. But be careful: Research has shown that remote work can produce the same negative hate points as in-person work. Working from home has made many employees feel isolated and overworked.

✓ To create a true human experience that allows all stakeholders to embrace the Covid-19 economy, leaders need to communicate frequently with their employees, even if their plans have yet to fully solidify. Organizations that articulate clear and specific policies and approaches for the future workplace will see employee productivity and well-being rise.

CHAPTER 11

The Employee
Touchpoint Journey

Much has been written about the journey of your customers. In two of my best-selling books, *What Customers Crave* and *What Customers Hate*, I presented fresh new insights into the customer's touchpoint relationship with your brand. The core of the concept is this: At each of the five touchpoints, your customers have different expectations and experiences. You need to be aware of this and architect the customer's journey accordingly. From the first touch, which is before the customer has any substantive interaction with your brand or your people, to the last touch, which is after the sale when your customer is once again a "free agent" and may or may not choose to buy from you again, your relationship with your customer is evolving. It requires that you stay focused on the reality of the moment—not what you *hope* will happen or *think* should happen but what's *actually* happening with your customer.

The touchpoint journey with each of your employees is much the same, but in many ways even more volatile and fraught with risk. When you think about it, all customers have one commonality, in the sense that your transaction with them is always the same: they give you money and in return you provide them with your product or service. Some customers will spend more than others and their spending may influence your business strategy. But unless you have a very customer-centric B2B business, your customer is always on the *outside*, while you're on the *inside*. You don't have customers sitting in on your manager's meetings or hovering over the assembly line. Think about a business like a bank. In that case, you actually serve your customers from behind a protective screen, and if they tried to come around behind the counter, you'd call the police.

On the other hand, an employee is someone you bring into the company to work with you every day, shoulder to shoulder. Their job is to help the company reach its goals by either carrying out policy (for employees and managers) or making policy (leaders). In a typical consumer goods or services company, any single employee will have more influence on the success or failure of the enterprise than any single average customer.

This is why the employee touchpoint journey is critically important. You need to understand it and ensure that at every step your employee is happy and therefore productive.

The employee's journey with your company comprises a series of five stations or touchpoints. At each of these touchpoints, the employee and the company build a relationship through countless daily interactions. These interactions may be brief or prolonged. At every touchpoint, the company has the opportunity to create either a feeling of love and happiness by the employee or a feeling of hate.

The sum total of the employee experience over the five touchpoints—which may extend in time to cover many years—is the Net Employee Experience (NEX). This is the measurement of what the employee hated and loved across all five touchpoints.

As we know from the RealRatings system, Hatepoints are measured across four negative experiences: not good, bad, hated, really hated.

Lovepoints are measured across four positive experiences: unliked, liked, loved, really loved.

NEX represents the net total of the work experience for an employee, found by subtracting the Hatepoints from the Lovepoints to produce a score. This score is very useful because it's expressly asking what an employee didn't like and what he or she did like at a specific touchpoint. This provides actionable insights that an organization can use to rapidly fix the dislikes and significantly improve their NEX score.

In the following five sections, I'll reveal and discuss the five touchpoints and the risks and opportunities of each as they relate to the overall NEX score.

1. The Pre-Touch

The first touch is not really a touch at all, but the awareness of your business in the mind of the future employee.

During some period in the past, your future employee had no knowledge of your company or your products, and therefore no opinion of it. This general lack of awareness may have lasted for a few years into childhood, or well into adult life. What's the first brand name that infants learn about? My guess is that for most little kids it's the Disney Company— and the company strives mightily to ensure the impression is positive. Remember, most people learn about companies first as consumers, and only later as prospective employees.

On the other hand, if your company is a start-up, then most of your prospective employees will have no prior knowledge of you. If in 1998 you asked software engineers and coders if they had heard of an internet company named "Google," the vast majority would have replied, "Google? No." Back then, the business had just two partners—Larry Page and Sergey Brin. The very first employee they hired was Craig Silverstein, a fellow PhD student at Stanford. By 2021, the company had nearly 140,000 employees working in 78 offices in more than 50 countries worldwide. These days, if you haven't heard of Google, you've probably been living in a cave with no internet.

The pre-touch phase may last for years if your company is a ubiquitous brand name like Ford or Apple. These are names that we learned about as kids, and they've lasted long enough so that they're still relevant (unlike Oldsmobile, Pan Am, Borders Books, and other venerable brands that have vanished). Or the pre-touch phase may last for a very short period of time, between when your future employee sees your job listing on Indeed.com and thinks, "XYZ Company? Never heard of them, but they're looking for someone with my qualifications," and when they walk in for their first interview.

Many companies make efforts to project a positive image to potential employees, especially those like Walmart that must hire thousands of new employees every year. Such campaigns tend to ramp up when the economy is hot and the unemployment rate is low. Then when a recession hits, companies shed jobs, and labor becomes cheap, suddenly it doesn't matter so much!

Much of what prospective employees think about a company is out of its direct control because opinions are formed on the basis of news reports and social media. If you go back to our discussion about the railroad industry in America, companies like Norfolk Southern and Union Pacific have social media reputations that—deserved or not—make them sound like terrible places to work. They can certainly influence their social media brand, and they should, but ultimately the power resides with employees and customers. If you're looking for a career in railroads, their big competitor, BNSF, has a far better reputation, and you'd probably make it your first choice.

Companies can change their reputations. Comcast was once one of the most loathed companies in America, and consumers equated it with the dark and creepy 1996 Jim Carrey comedy *The Cable Guy*. In 2004 and 2007, the American Customer Satisfaction Index (ACSI) survey found that Comcast had the worst customer satisfaction rating of any company or government agency in the country, including the Internal Revenue Service.

But by 2020, a massive internal effort had turned the company around. That year's ACSI survey found Comcast's Xfinity brand was the "most improved" overall, and especially saw a "staggering improvement" in satisfaction with its pay TV service. The employees seem reasonably happy too—in December 2021, the company scored a respectable 3.9 rating out of 5 on CareerBliss.com, a 3.8 on Glassdoor, and a 3.7 on Indeed.com.

How do you manage your reputation in the marketplace of potential customers, investors, and employees? That could easily be the subject for an entire book, so suffice to say you need to fight the war on two fronts:

- Your company must actually be a good place to work. You must strive to instill the Happiness Principle at every level and in every cubicle and workstation. It must be real and not just a public relations scam. Thanks to social media, companies are increasingly transparent. What happens in the office quickly becomes public.

   In July 2021, a video went viral on TikTok, receiving over 3.7 million views, nearly 550,000 likes, and thousands of comments. Posted by "amazonassociatef1," it was filmed when workers at an Amazon fulfillment center headed for break at 9:59, which was one minute early. A disembodied voice booms out over the loudspeaker, "It's 9:59, not ten o'clock, guys. If you are on your way to break you are getting TOT as we speak!"

   "TOT" stands for "time off task," something Amazon will deem an unpaid break and not compensate employees for.[1]

   Episodes such as this one served to draw public attention to the fact that warehouse bathrooms can be located as distant as a 10-minute walk from a worker's station. This makes it nearly impossible for these employees to use the restroom during a 15-minute break.

   Even more dehumanizing than the Orwellian tracking was the fact that the supervisor yelled at the employees over a loudspeaker rather than personally speaking with them to find out what was going on.

- You need to stay in touch with your potential labor pool. Aside from actually being a happy place to work, you need to ensure that your story is being told. You need to be on top of social media and know what's being said.

   Let's face it—if you have 100 employees, then it's likely that one of them will take a swipe at you on Glassdoor or Indeed.

That's just the way life is! It happens to the best of companies. But if a highly qualified prospective employee checks out your company's reviews and sees one or more negative one-star reviews, he or she won't be swayed by them if they see 99 others that are positive, and if your overall rating is high.

Every company of every size needs a social media director. If your company is a sole proprietorship, then that person will be you. You'll need to create your social media presence. This means learning about the various platforms—Facebook, Instagram, Twitter, Snapchat, even TikTok—as well as the employment websites.

As you add employees, you can shift the burden. A professional full-time social media manager will cost you an average of $80,000 a year, depending on your location.

2. The Interviews

Let's say you're looking to fill an executive-level position. The person in this leadership job will wield enough responsibility and power to materially affect the current and future performance of the company. For whatever reason, it's not being filled internally, so you need to search outside the company.

The process is neither simple nor cheap.

Your goal is to attract the best possible "happy warrior" you can. In a growing economy, competition for the best executive talent is keen, and you may have to sell your company to the candidate as much as they need to sell themselves to you. Aside from the mechanical stuff like placing ads and hiring headhunters, you need to design an interview process that will give the right candidate a very good feeling about the organization and its direction.

You'll probably form a search committee to identify, screen, and interview prospective employees. This job may also be initiated by your human resources department, or in a small company by the person who will manage the newcomer.

It goes without saying that your personal behavior must always be cordial, respectful, and businesslike. And I'm sure you know about the federal and state regulations governing the types of questions you can ask. But in addition, you need to be able to tell the candidate *why* you need them and *what* you want them to do. This will give both parties the opportunity to discuss the specifics of the role and how the candidate can contribute to the success of the organization.

Be sure to leverage the input from the search committee to reach consensus on what you're looking for. To ensure the picture you paint for the candidate is crystal clear, use the following MOC framework. Some people call it a candidate profile or job spec, which are the same thing. The goal is to define what you want in these three areas:

- **Mission.** What do you need this person to do over the next year or two? Describe the essence of the job's daily activities in one page or less. Unless the job is technical, like software coding, use plain English, not business mumbo-jumbo. Be sure to specify the amount and type of support and collaboration the new hire can expect to receive.
- **Outcomes.** As the result of the person's work, what well-defined deliverables are you looking for? Ranked by order of importance,

list the specific and measurable business outcomes you expect as a result of the mission.

- **Competencies.** In order to execute the mission and deliver the outcomes, what specific experiences, skills, and accomplishments should they have? Which of these are critical attributes and which are optional? These decisions should flow from the mission and outcomes.

Everyone's input should be consolidated into the initial draft of the MOC, and then have the hiring committee meet in person to review the draft.

If possible, have the company CEO personally reach out to the top candidates with a brief, friendly email. This personal connection, which says "you are important to us," can often mean the difference between your top candidate choosing you rather than your competitor.

During the interviews themselves—for high-level positions there will be several—after you've told the candidate what you're looking for, ask them for what *they're* looking for. Many seemingly happy hirings have quickly soured because the interview process failed to reveal the true personality and aspirations of the candidate. Be sure you're not projecting onto the candidate what you *want* them to be, rather than seeing them for who they really are.

Hiring for executive positions can be costly. Expenses you'll be paying may include advertising the opening, the time costs of an internal recruiter, the recruiter's assistant in reviewing résumés and performing other recruitment-related tasks, and the person conducting the interviews; drug screens and background checks; job fair and campus recruiting costs; and various pre-employment assessment tests. If you use an outside recruiter, you can add third-party fees, such as agencies, travel expenses for recruitment, applicant tracking system (ATS) fees, and aptitude test providers.

According to data published by The Hire Talent, a talent assessment company, hiring an entry-level employee is estimated to cost 20 percent of that employee's annual salary. Hiring a mid-level employee typically runs up an average cost of $60,000, or as much as 1.5 times the employee's salary. To hire an executive-level employee typically costs a US company more than 200 percent of the new executive's salary to complete the hiring and onboarding process.[2]

At the end of the day, after your candidate has completed the entire interview process, the goal should be to have a candidate who thinks to themselves, "I hope they call me with good news. I really want to work there!"

3. Onboarding and Training

You can interview a candidate over and over again, get their references, and give them tests, but the ultimate proof lies in just one thing: Bringing the person into your company and making them part of your team.

The process cannot be haphazard. You can't just make it up as you go along. Because how you handle the first few days and months of a new employee's experience is crucial to ensuring high retention, onboarding new hires should be a strategic process that lasts at least one year.

Successful onboarding covers four key areas:

1. **Social.** The new employee needs to feel welcome, be able to build and promote productive relationships with colleagues and managers and become a valued part of the organization.
2. **Operational.** The new employee needs the right tools, materials, and knowledge (such as clarity and business jargon) to do their job well.
3. **Strategic.** The new employee needs to know the mission, vision, and goals of the organization and identify with them.
4. **Ethical.** He or she needs to know the organization's standards of behavior and how they are expected to treat customers, colleagues, and subordinates.

To ensure your new employee is happy, take steps to minimize confusion and uncertainty while maximizing confidence and clarity. Provide an onboarding portal with content designed to engage them, like first-day information, a friendly note from their manager, welcome messages and photos from new teammates, a glossary of company acronyms, a virtual copy of your employee handbook, and information about the nuts and bolts of everyday operations, beginning with where they can park their car and how the phone system works.

Every new hire needs a mentor or guide who's responsible for answering questions and "showing them the ropes." If their immediate supervisor is not able to do it, then it needs to be a fellow team member.

Effective onboarding practices should reflect well on the company's brand. In the first weeks of starting a new job, friends, family, and former colleagues will ask the person about their new employer. You want this first impression to be as positive as possible. With proper onboarding, new employees will immediately share a good impression of the company within their direct network.

That's what you want! Happiness through and through. But despite your best efforts, it can be difficult to know if a new employee is truly happy. Some people will tell you they're perfectly happy right up until the moment they quit. This is because they want to hold onto that power. They may be afraid that if they bring up a problem or say something negative, the company might let them go or somehow penalize them. They want to be able to make that choice, not the company.

Welcome Them—and Then Pay Them to Quit

There are two ways to solve this problem. You probably should do both.

The first way is to welcome the new hire to your organizational family. Show them a culture of happiness, self-analysis, and constructive criticism. The new hire will either accept it and become engaged, or will remain suspicious and aloof, hiding their true feelings.

The second way is to make quitting as easy as possible. You can do this by offering them cash to leave.

The practice came to the public's attention in 2004, when Tony Hsieh, founder and CEO of online shoe retailer Zappos, announced that after a week or so on the job, new employees could take a $1,000 payoff to quit. It became known as "The Offer," and when people thought about it, the idea made sense. It's well known that an unhappy employee can be a financial drain on a company due to low productivity and more frequent mistakes, so it made sense to pay the unhappy employee a small portion of what they cost the company and be rid of them. Soon, The Offer was increased to $4,000.

The Offer also had an effect on employees who chose to stay. Employees who declined the offer were psychologically recommitting to the company. This made them more engaged, more productive, and ultimately boosted the company's bottom line.

As Zappos training manager Rachael Brown told the American Management Association, "The people who do take The Offer are so thankful that we understand that this just isn't the right place for them. But the employees who *don't* take it are very committed. They go home and they come back with these great stories about how they told their family about this crazy offer that Zappos asked them to quit today, and they definitely come back with a sense of commitment."[3]

In 2009, Amazon acquired Zappos, along with The Offer. In his 2014 annual letter to shareholders, Amazon founder Jeff Bezos explained the company had added a program modeled after the one started by Zappos CEO Tony Hsieh. After some tweaking, Bezos and Amazon titled the program "Pay to Quit." The program worked differently than at Zappos. Rather than receiving the offer once during training, employees at Amazon's fulfillment centers can claim the offer once a year, in February, following the holiday rush. In the employee's first year the offer is for $2,000. The amount then increases by $1,000 each year to a maximum of $5,000, where it remains. The idea is that the longer an unhappy employee stays, the more entrenched they become, and so it would take a bigger offer to dislodge them.

"We want people working at Amazon who want to be here," Amazon spokesperson Melanie Etches told CNBC *Make It*. "In the long-term, staying somewhere you don't want to be isn't healthy for our employees or for the company."[4]

Of course, Amazon being Amazon, there's more to their offer than meets the eye.

Many analysts believe Amazon benefits from The Offer more than you might think. While it removes employees who are unsatisfied with their position and who may not be giving their all to the company, it also saves the company money in the long run.

The company has long made it clear that fulfillment center jobs should be high turnover. They *want* you to quit after a year or two. The churn allows the company to replace older workers with fresh new hires at starting wage with no benefits. It saves the company money in stock payouts, 401k payouts, vacation pay, regular and overtime pay, VCP payments, and other benefits.

This means that while Amazon incurs a relatively small expense when paying for workers to quit, in the end the savings to the company more than make up for the initial loss.

Here's the bottom line: If you truly want a happy worker, then when you bring him or her into your organization, don't just say, "Sink or swim." That's not productive. Instead, treat them like family. Show them some love and prove that you want them to succeed. Model respect and good teamwork.

4. The Mid-Career Touchpoint

You need employees who are loyal, happy, and want to stay with your company.

To be more specific, you want a robust complement of two distinct types of employees:

1. The Leader, who wants to climb the corporate ladder and eventually assume a position of leadership, either as CEO or on the executive team. The quintessential examples are CEOs like Mary Barra (GM), Doug McMillon (Walmart), and Chris Rondeau (Planet Fitness). These and many more very happy leaders started at the very bottom of their companies and worked their way up to the top.

2. The Homemaker, who does not aspire to leadership but instead wants to rise to a certain level of responsibility and stay there. There are many good people who are happy workers who don't want the responsibility of running the company or planning for an uncertain future. Such people can be invaluable in terms of "organizational memory" and providing continuity; but they may also be resistant to change. They may have outside interests, such as church, family, or a hobby, and look at their job as a way of providing for their family and having a respectable community identity.

Of course, you need the other types as well, but they're likely to be more transient.

To keep mid-career employees happy, you need to provide a few things.

- **Loyalty.** They're ready to extend loyalty when they feel they're getting it in return.
- **Respect.** While many mid-career Homemaker types aren't interested in shouldering increasing responsibilities, they absolutely want their service to be respected. If they have an opinion, they want it to be heard and acknowledged.
- **A Happy Workplace.** If your job is a steppingstone to something else, you'll endure more hate points because you know you're just passing through. But if you're going to spend a good chunk of your life at one company, you need to feel happy about coming to work in the morning. And it's not about free bagels in the break room; remember the formula:

$$\text{Work} + \text{Recreation} + \text{Meaning} = \text{Happy Work}$$

When you have the right mix, you'll have an employee who's not thinking about jumping ship.
- **Competitive Pay.** Anyone who chooses to work for one company at the same level for years knows they're not going to

get rich. You can safely assume that such workers are not driven solely by the quest for more money. They have other things that are important to them. Respect this, and don't take it for granted. Pay—including profit sharing—that keeps pace with the competition is very important.

- **Lifelong Learning.** Every company experiences disruption while (hopefully) fostering innovation. Each and every employee needs to be provided with the appropriate training and education to maintain the flexibility and strength of the company through periods of change. This helps the organization perform better and staves off the boredom that inevitably comes from doing the same thing for long periods of time.

For Leaders who seek to climb the executive ladder, you need to provide an upward route. Obviously, this will have limitations. Every organization resembles a pyramid, with increasingly fewer opportunities as you ascend higher. Not every Leader can find a role for themselves! You need to have clear plans of succession so that when (for example) a vice president leaves for another firm that offers a leadership role, you've got a manager ready to take the promotion and fill the role that will be vacant.

Mentorship can be an important asset for grooming future leaders. In a program of leadership development coaching, a good mentor can help a subordinate or younger executive come out of his or her comfort zone by creating different leadership scenarios.

Mentors can provide specific insights and information that enable the mentee's success. They can also help in networking and introduce the mentee to the people and organizations they'll need to interact with as they climb the organizational ladder.

Even better, the benefits of mentoring go both ways. While leadership mentoring is primarily for the benefit of the mentees, by giving back to the people in their organization, leaders who choose to mentor others derive personal fulfillment through their contributions. They may also find it rewarding to see the employees they mentor succeed in their careers.

5. Post-Retirement

Many leaders foolishly think, "After Smith or Jones retires, what do I care about them? They're gone. They're ancient history." This is very short-sighted thinking. It pays to stay on good terms with them, because you never know when you might need them.

During the waning of the Covid-19 pandemic as workplaces tried to ramp up to full speed, suddenly employers experienced a severe labor shortage. This crisis—the term is not used lightly—was caused by a variety of conditions that, like a perfect storm, all came together at once: worker disillusionment with their former jobs, aversion to commuting again, fear of Covid infection, lack of affordable childcare, and many schools operating remotely. In a tight labor market, many employers sought every solution when seeking to fill open positions. Many turned to their own former employees and other retirees. According to Rand Corporation, of workers who were age 65 or older, 40 percent had retired at least once before.[5]

According to a study conducted by job search platform Resume Builder, 20 percent of retirees said past employers asked them to return because of the labor shortage. And while 41 percent said they would consider going back to their former position, 59 percent indicated they wanted to seek employment elsewhere.

Of those who didn't want to return to their former employer, a majority said they wanted to switch industries, with the most common reasons being less stress, the ability to work remotely, and switching to a career they were more interested in.[6]

Some retirees returned to work because they needed money to pay their bills, while others used their paycheck for travel, hobbies, or leisure activities. Many wanted to work because they found it fulfilling and a more appealing alternative to other retirement options.

By bringing back a retired employee, companies can save time on training and compensation. Retirees returning to the company reduces the need to recruit for an employee who would have to learn the company's processes. It also allows employers to pay retirees a reduced rate, since it's often unnecessary for them to be employed full time and they're probably taking Social Security.

Oh, and what about the idea that older employees are resistant to learning new techniques and approaches? As Alison Pearson, head of HR at a personal injury law firm in Pittsburgh told SHRM, "There's a stereotype that the older an employee, the less likely they are able to adapt to technology and grow with the company. But in my experience, that's a lazy perspective."[7]

Older workers may also have years of experience in a variety of career fields, which can make them more versatile than younger workers who are just starting out in their chosen field. A highly experienced older worker can serve as a mentor and be an invaluable source of knowledge to support younger workers.

Your former employees are a valuable "reserve force" that can help you when you need them. It's all the more reason to make them happy in the years *before* they retire!

Take Action!

✓ The employee's journey with your company comprises a series of five stations or touchpoints. It's critically important that you understand it and ensure that at every step your employee is happy and therefore productive.

✓ The sum total of the employee experience over the five touchpoints—which may extend in time to cover many years—is the Net Employee Experience (NEX).

✓ The five touchpoints are:

1. **The Pre-Touch**, which is the awareness of your business in the mind of the future employee.

2. **The Interviews.** You need to design an interview process that will give the right

candidate a very good feeling about the organization and its direction.

3. **Onboarding and Training.** How you handle the first few days and months of a new employee's experience is crucial to ensuring high retention. Onboarding new hires should be a strategic process that lasts at least one year. You may even want to consider a "pay to quit" offer.

4. **The Mid-Career Touchpoint.** To keep these employees happy, you need to provide loyalty, respect, a happy workplace, competitive pay, lifelong learning. For Leaders who seek to climb the executive ladder, you need to provide an upward route.

5. **Post-Retirement.** It pays to stay on good terms with your retired employees, because you never know when you might need them. Your former employees are a valuable "reserve force" that can help you when you need them.

CHAPTER 12

Innovation and Employee Experience Design

In my professional work, my clients and colleagues know me as the "innovation guy." This implies that the focus of my work is helping leaders and organizations *ride the waves of the future*. My clients and I tackle tough subjects like seeing emerging trends, leveraging industry disruption, and taking advantage of the increasing rate of change in the marketplace.

Perhaps not surprisingly, the question I get often is, "Why is the innovation guy spending his time working with organizations to help them improve their employee and customer experiences *today?*"

The answer is simple: Employee and customer happiness is an innovation activity that both improves your organization *today* and positions it for a brighter, more profitable *tomorrow*.

Let's start with a definition of innovation.

Innovation is the creation of *novel value that serves your organization and your customer*.

Let's dissect the anatomy of this definition:

Novel simply means "new," and in a time of massive change we need to constantly find new ways to build new value for our customers and employees.

"Value" is the tangible contribution we provide to the community or market we serve. It's something that helps people live better lives, gives shelter, nourishment, or health, or simply provides them with entertainment to brighten their day.

"Your organization and your customer" is the human ecosystem composed of people with whom we work and to whom we deliver products and services. By delivering value to the customer, we help them; but it's also good to create value for our organization in the sense that if the organization becomes bigger, stronger, or more efficient, it can better serve its customers and stakeholders.

Innovation—both enterprise and customer—needs a target, and the target of innovation for organizations are all of the humans that it serves. The better an organization is at coming up with ideas and deploying on those ideas in a way that delivers value to the enterprise and the customer, the more likely is the success of the organization.

So now the only question is how we institutionalize innovation in a way that consistently targets employee happiness, enterprise growth, and customer satisfaction. This is an interesting concept because innovation means change, and so how do you then make "change" a permanent part of your organization's existence? Many leaders like to think that they need to make the organization a finely tuned machine that, once perfected, will keep running indefinitely, and that if "something ain't broke, don't fix it." They say, "Making the business profitable the first time is a tough enough job, so once it is profitable, I'm not going to mess around with it!"

Instead of this static model, it's better to think of an organization like an airplane. Building it and getting it off the ground the first time takes a lot of work, but once it's airborne, the trick is to *keep* it airborne. You need to constantly adjust for wind and weather; while you may be able to put it on autopilot for brief periods, as a long-term solution that's not going to work. If you don't pay attention to changing conditions, you might find yourself crashing into the side of a mountain.

In my best-selling book *The Innovation Mandate*, I outlined the importance of building a thoughtful and robust *innovation pipeline* that allows you to generate, evaluate, deploy, and manage useful ideas that support the happiness of your culture. In this chapter I'm going to provide a light and airy approach to building an innovation infrastructure that allows you to get ideas and move them through a pipeline. This approach has two very important features.

Your Employees Are Innovators

Your employees are natural innovators, and they want to have the opportunity to collaborate and cocreate. This is one of the most important ways in which we improve the quality and meaning of work life for employees. Leveraging internal social networks—sometimes referred to as enterprise social networks—you can set up innovation challenges and allow your employees to help you eliminate waste, improve customer experience, or anything else that you would like to accomplish. It can be done by collaborating in cocreating with your employees. The importance of this approach cannot be overstated, as employees want to know they're involved in the authorship of the systems, tools, and processes that they use every day in their work. We use the term inclusive a lot today, but the term is about allowing people to be included and that means in a very practical way. They want to be included in the creation and movement of ideas.

My Little Secret

Do you want to know a secret? For over three decades, I've been a strategic advisor serving some of the top brands in the world. While every challenge is different and requires different solutions, the ultimate goal is always the same: to help companies improve their profitability. Thankfully, my clients are consistently happy with my work. Why? It's not because of me! It's because the amazing people who work within my clients' organizations are willing to share with me their ideas, problems, and opportunities. They give me insights about the lay of the land, the problems they face, and ideas on how to fix them.

For some reason, too many employers don't accept advice from their incredible employees. Instead, they're glad to pay me for my advice. That's fine with me! I suppose it's somehow more acceptable if a neutral third party (me) comes in, talks to the employees confidentially, gathers their ideas, and submits them to leadership. It's a win-win for everyone.

I think it's time that we really start respecting the internal genius that we have within our organizations by building out an innovation infrastructure that allows them to help us drive quality of work life and growth.

Innovation Creates Happiness, Which Creates More Innovation

Employee productivity is the backbone of any organization's success, and happier employees are more productive. And what gives human beings the most satisfaction and deep internal happiness? Creating something new that has value.

It's a virtuous cycle. Research has shown that human beings tend to become happy and derive satisfaction from activities that result in the creation of something new of value. Have you ever seen a child proudly show her new drawing to her parents or teacher? The child says, "Look! I drew a picture of a house and a sun in the sky!" Her happiness in palpable. We may grow up to be serious adults, but our delight in creating something new never leaves us.

The cycle begins when the happiness at having created something new then spurs us to do it again. Happy people tend to be more interested in exploring new solutions to difficult problems.

And we're not talking about geniuses being the sole sources of innovation. That's a myth. While there are some people who are truly exceptional, the vast majority of innovations come from ordinary rank-and-file employees. Reality shows us that under the right circumstances, anyone with normal human capacities is capable of producing creative work.

Another myth is that creativity somehow impedes productivity. Again, reality shows us that for complex work in organizations, there is no trade-off between creativity and productivity, efficiency, or work quality.

Harvard professor Teresa M. Amabile has done significant research on how the work environment can influence the motivation, creativity, and performance of individuals and teams. As she told *Harvard Business Review*, if a person is in a good mood on a given day, they're more likely to have creative ideas that day, as well as the next day, even if we take into account their mood that next day. When people are feeling good, a cognitive process leads to more flexible, fluent, and original thinking, and there's actually a carryover, an incubation effect, to the next day.

Not surprisingly, she found the behavior of the team leader is critical. She's identified four distinct leader behaviors that have a positive influence on the feelings—and therefore the performance—of subordinates. They are:

1. Supporting people emotionally.
2. Monitoring people's work in a particularly positive way, and giving them positive feedback on their work or giving them information that they need to do their work better.
3. Recognizing people for good performance, particularly in public settings.
4. Consulting with people on the team—that is, asking for their views, respecting their opinions, and acting on their needs and their wishes to the extent that it's possible.

Avoid These Seven Common Pitfalls

The upsides of a happy culture are even better than I could ever describe in this book. They positively impact every aspect of your organization, your employees, and the customers you serve. A campaign to promote Happy Work and make it a vital part of company culture should be effective and produce results that you can measure.

With that being said, it's important to make certain you avoid the seven common pitfalls that can result from an organization's failure to achieve the robust cultural transformation it needs to sustain happiness day after day, year after year:

1. It's Just a Box to Check

Many employee happiness initiatives collapse because the CEO was never really committed to it in the first place! They look at "happiness" and "quality of work life" as a box they know they're supposed to check. This is one of the major reasons why ordinary efforts don't work. The CEO simply didn't commit the resources, time, and the philosophy of happiness to giving it a fighting chance.

2. It's Poisoned by WIIFM

Another common problem with attempts at cultural transformation is that organizations and leaders often view it from the perspective of "What's in it for me?" (also known as WIIFM). Happiness cultures are based on the philosophy of *serving others*, and that is the primary focus. Once you attempt to catalog the daily enterprise benefits without putting your stakeholders, employees, and customers first, your initiative simply won't work.

3. Ouch! They Stop Because It Hurts

Short-term pain is often necessary for long-term gain. Change of any type is painful at some level for a while. Transitioning from a traditional culture to one that puts happiness and humanity first is guaranteed to cause some disruption. My advice to my clients is to accept the fact that cultural transformation can be disorienting, disruptive, and even painful, and it often takes longer than one would expect. If you know this going into the initiative, you'll be far better prepared to stay the course in order to reap the amazing benefits.

4. It's Fractional

In what I call "The Vested Ecosystem" (VE), everyone whom you and your organization will impact, and everyone within your ecosystem, must be served across their entire journey and across a range of personality personas.

Unfortunately, many organizations attempt to impact a small portion of their overall VE, and as a result they never really reach the goal of sustained happiness. Additionally, many organizations do not use complete systems, processes, and tools that are necessary to drive a dynamic and happy enterprise, and as a result their initiative loses steam and ultimately fails. This really speaks to the importance of building out a formal Happiness as a Strategy plan that is hardwired to your entire enterprise strategy.

5. It's Mono-Directional

Many organizations see all enterprise initiatives as something that they author and deploy onto their stakeholders. This "mono-directional" ("one-way") approach is flawed on many levels, and as a result it never works. One of the keys to employee happiness is the ability to consistently listen to and collaborate with your customers, employees, and stakeholders. Your employees want to be part of the discussion. They also want to be part of the decision making. Remember the best innovations that will help your organization thrive is in the heads of your employees, and if allowed they want to share it with you.

6. It's Vague

One of the most important structures of a happiness initiative is the communication strategy embraced by the CEO. This strategy must provide ongoing, clear messaging on how employees can participate in the organization's journey to happiness and personal meeting. Unfortunately, many leaders see communication as incidental and a one-way broadcast. Building out a two-way initiative communication strategy as well as a CEO communication strategy is critical to taking the amorphous and squishy concept of happiness and making it an enterprise reality.

7. It's Contradictory

In my global management consulting practice, I have seen this phenomenon occur too many times. A CEO talks about the importance of happiness and humanity, all the while creating policies and behaviors that are completely contradictory to those proclamations. (You can probably think of more than one well-known CEO who does this!) But you don't have to be perfect, and admitting your imperfection early on is a powerful way to get stakeholder adoption. Be honest with your employees, talk about what's not right, and then commit to collaborating and listening to them to create new humanistic approach toward building a fair, equitable, and beautiful work environment.

Take Action!

- ✓ Employee and customer happiness is an innovation activity that both improves your organization today and positions it for a brighter, more profitable tomorrow.
- ✓ Think of your organization like an airplane. Building it and getting it off the ground the first time takes a lot of work, but once it's airborne, the trick is to keep it airborne. You need to constantly adjust for wind and weather; while you may be able to put it on autopilot for brief periods, as a long-term solution that's not going to work. If you don't pay attention to changing conditions, you might find yourself crashing into the side of a mountain.
- ✓ Your employees are natural innovators, and they want to have the opportunity to collaborate and cocreate.
- ✓ Remember the virtuous cycle: Human beings tend to become happy and derive satisfaction from activities that result in the creation of something new of value. The cycle begins when the happiness at having created something new then spurs us to do it again.

CHAPTER 13

The Leader's Guide to Making Workplace Happiness Real

It goes without saying that a happy workplace is a more productive and profitable workplace. Happy employees are willing to go the extra mile to succeed, are better team players, and genuinely care about their customers. They connect with customers who are ready to spend more money at a happy company.

Given the advantages of a happy workplace, there's simply no rational reason to tolerate a company culture that's toxic (at worst) or mediocre and boring (at best). Such a workplace will slowly decline, lose profitability, suffer the exit of top employees, and eventually get bought for pennies on the dollar.

But the busy CEO may ask, how can I cultivate a happy company in real life? The task seems overwhelming. I don't know where to start.

This is a good question. Fortunately, we know that transformative results come from good questions.

The answer begins with a plan of action. It's a road map that's been proven to take you where you want to go. A step-by-step set of instructions that you can follow, no matter how busy or distracted you may be.

159

This is your road map. Take it one step at a time, and you'll see the results you want. You might even look like a hero to your investors and customers!

Ready? Let's get started!

1. Define Happiness

If I said to you, "To succeed in business, you must get a baslop. That is your goal."

Your first response would be, "What the heck is a baslop? Please define it."

That makes perfect sense. You can't possibly set a goal without first knowing what the goal is.

If the goal is to be happy at work, we first need to agree on what that means. Let's begin with some research. Dictionary.com tells us, *happy* is an adjective. In ordinary usage, it means:

- Delighted, pleased, or glad, as over a particular thing: *to be happy it's Friday.*
- Characterized by or indicative of pleasure, contentment, or joy: *a happy mood; a happy frame of mind.*

Over the centuries, people have debated the meaning of true, deepdown happiness. In his book *Happiness: A History,* Darrin M. McMahon reminds us that for the ancient Greeks, happiness was the result of virtue. If you were not virtuous, you stood little chance of being happy. For the Romans, it sprang from prosperity and divine favor. Therefore, it was difficult to be poor and happy.

Throughout history, happiness has been seen as the most perfect human state, and not necessarily a momentary emotion that could come and go as circumstances changed. In the modern era, we've begun to think of happiness as not just an earthly possibility but also as an entitlement, even an obligation.[1]

The Declaration of Independence guarantees the right to "life, liberty, and the pursuit of happiness." Most scholars now agree the words "the pursuit" do not mean to chase after happiness, as if to catch, but to simply *be* happy. In the Declaration, the pursuit of happiness is not a quest or something you seek, but "an unalienable right." Everyone has the right to actually *be* happy, not just *try* to be happy.

Happiness can mean many things to many people. Psychologist Tchiki Davis, founder of The Berkeley Well-Being Institute, conducted a survey in which people were asked what factors contributed to their happiness. They could choose more than one. The eleven factors included:

- **Self-awareness.** The ability to attend to and acknowledge thoughts, emotions, and behaviors.
- **Self-regulation.** The ability to control and manage thoughts, emotions, and behaviors.
- **Gratitude.** The tendency to be thankful for people, experiences, and things, and to show appreciation for the kindness of others.
- **Empathy.** The ability to understand and share the feelings of another person.
- **Assertiveness.** The ability to be self-assured in advocating for your own needs.
- **Resilience.** The capacity to cope with or recover quickly from difficult events.
- **Positive thinking.** The capacity to have attitudes that focus on the bright side of things.
- **Social skills.** The ability to interact and communicate with others in effective and successful ways.
- **Conscientiousness.** The tendency to be faithful, loyal, and responsible.
- **Kindness.** The virtue of benevolence, compassion, and humanity.
- **Wisdom.** Knowledge that can be acquired through study or learning from others.[2]

The answers were surprisingly uniform, with all the factors receiving a similar number of votes. The lowest vote-getter, assertiveness, was chosen by about 50 percent of the respondents, while the top vote-getter, positive thinking, was chosen by about 70 percent of the respondents. Clearly, in ordinary circumstances, there are many ways to arrive at happiness, and we share many of those ways in common.

To take one more pass at defining happiness, here are a few quotes from learned people about the subject:

- "Happiness consists more in conveniences of pleasure that occur every day than in great pieces of good fortune that happen but seldom." —Benjamin Franklin
- "Happiness is not an ideal of reason, but of imagination." —Immanuel Kant
- "There can be no happiness if the things we believe in are different from the things we do." —Freya Stark

And one of my personal favorites:

- "If you want happiness for an hour, take a nap. If you want happiness for a day, go fishing. If you want happiness for a year, inherit a fortune. If you want happiness for a lifetime, help someone else." —Chinese proverb

We could go on and on, but you get the idea.

For our purposes, here's how I define happiness on the job:

"The engagement of purposeful work that serves our personal growth, in a way that positively impacts and serves others."

You can see it has three main components. You'll be happy at work if you (1) do something constructive that (2) enriches you and (3) produces something good for other people.

If you miss one of the three, you may not be happy. For example, let's say you work in a fast-food restaurant. Your job is to flip burgers for eight hours a day.

It's clear you're (1) doing something constructive and (3) producing something good for other people. But how about personal enrichment? That could go one of several ways:

- If you're nothing more than a human robot and you have no authority and no control over your work, and you have no other employment prospects, you will probably become bored and miserable.
- If you see your fast-food job as an entry-level steppingstone to a manager's role or even higher, or you intend to learn the business and then open your own franchise, then you might be very happy.
- If you're a college kid and it's a temporary summer job to earn extra cash and gain an interesting life experience, you might be very happy.

Different people can look at the same job in different ways. One burger-flipper might be miserable, while another might be very happy. Here's the part that should matter to you, the leader: *You* can look at the same job in different ways. How your employees view their jobs depends a lot upon how *you* view their jobs. If you want miserable employees, you shall have them. If you want happy employees, you can have them.

You want happy employees.

2. Listen, Learn, and Collaborate

You've decided that your goal as a leader is to create a work culture where your stakeholders are engaged in purposeful work that serves their personal growth, in a way that positively impacts and serves others.

You've made a very positive decision!

Having figured out where you want to *go*, the next step is to determine *where you are now*. A map is useless unless you know your starting point.

For an organization, "where you are now" means determining the relative level of stakeholder happiness.

Yes, it's a tricky thing to do. It's not like taking inventory in your warehouse or adding up your quarterly revenues. Those are easily quantifiable. They exist as numbers.

Happiness is qualitative. This makes it a bit more challenging, but no less important than the other metrics. And if you use the RealRatings system, from the qualitative analysis you can generate a set of numbers that you can then compare over time to see if they rise or fall.

The first task is to *listen*. This is where many CEOs have trouble. They're accustomed to charting the course and getting stakeholders on board by cajoling and convincing. They tend to be very good at persuasion, but not so good at listening.

Here's how you do it. As a leader, whether your company is B2B or B2C, you're probably very good at listening to your customers. In order to stay in business, you have to be! Your customers do not hesitate to tell you what makes them happy. They tell you on social media and they tell you when they call to make a complaint. In some industries, such as autos and home electronics, independent reviewers will write reviews and publish them. You can also use surveys to gauge customer satisfaction. And, of course, they vote with their pocketbooks. Taken together, all of these sources of feedback give you a good idea of the level of happiness of your customers.

Your stakeholders, including your employees, are your customers too. They choose to work for you and support the company. They "buy" their paychecks with their time and talent. If they're not happy, they'll look to buy their paychecks somewhere else.

As you approach the task of listening to your stakeholders—which should be an ongoing activity for as long as you hold your job—the key is to *eliminate your preconceptions.* You must open your eyes and ears to what you really see and hear, not what you *want* to see or hear or *think you ought* to see or hear.

Don't take it personally. Too many CEOs respond to stakeholder comments as if they were personal insults. They think like King Louis XIV of France, the "Sun King," who is the reported originator of the phrase *"L'état, c'est moi"*—"The state, it is I." If you feel this way, you need to get over it. With leadership comes responsibility, and one of those responsibilities includes always doing the right thing for your stakeholders, even if it means humbling yourself.

Use a combination of listening sessions and anonymous surveys to determine the current state of employee love and hate. Our RealRating system is designed to identify those sentiments across the entire employee journey. I would recommend using something that identifies current states of satisfaction across archetypes, touchpoints, and other key determinants. It's important to realize that if you want great insights, it's a little bit more work in the beginning to conduct ideation sessions and listening sessions, but you will get better information and ultimately have a much better result.

The second task is to *learn*. It's not enough to listen with open ears. You then need to put what you're hearing into context and identify courses of action.

Let's say you lead a big hospital. You do a RealRatings survey of your front-line intake staff—the people who greet patients as they arrive for nonemergency treatment. They tell you the number one complaint of patients is the excessive wait time in the waiting room. The patients arrive for their appointment on time, and then have to wait. Especially in the era of Covid-19, patients hate sitting in a closed room with other sick people. Some may even get up and leave.

If you weren't interested in learning, you might respond by saying, "We can't help that. This is a hospital, where we heal people. If our patients can't wait a few minutes to be seen by our wonderful doctors, then they have a problem."

If you wanted to learn and improve your service to your patients—who are your customers—and also make your intake staff happier, you might say, "Let's set up an instant message system whereby we'd send a text message to the patient when it's time for them to check in. They could wait outside in their car, or even at home if they lived close by." It's a simple system already in use by many clinics. As soon as an examination room becomes available, you send a text to the next patient in line. They come in, get processed, and are whisked to the examination room within minutes. Everyone's happy!

The third task is to *collaborate*. This simply means that it's never enough for you, the leader, to announce a happiness program or initiative, tell people what to do, and then sit back and watch the results. Remember, this is a qualitative effort, not quantitative. It involves peoples' feelings, which directly impact their actions. The energy flow is in all directions—from you out to your employees, from your employees to your customers, from your customers back to the employees, and from one employee to another. The "vibe" of the organization goes round and round, amplifying itself here or diminishing there. What happens in sales may impact R&D, and what happens in human resources may impact finance. As CEO, your job it is to manage this energy flow to produce the highest level of stakeholder happiness possible.

3. Validate

You know the difference between *data* and *information*.

Data are unprocessed facts, numbers, and opinions. A data set is considered to be useless in its raw form. A mass of data is like iron ore—there's potential value there, but before you can produce usable iron or steel you need to put the raw iron ore through various smelting processes to remove the oxygen and other unwanted molecules. Similarly, data must be processed and put into context before it can be used as the basis for a business decision.

For example, let's say that raw data from year 1 at Company A shows that the average employee tenure was 4.5 years. What does that mean? In isolation, it means nothing. It's just a data point.

Let's put it into context. Let's say the average employee tenure at the top five firms in Company A's industry has consistently been 6 years. And let's also say that in the previous year, the average employee tenure at Company A was 5 years, and in the year before that it was 5.5 years.

Now we have actionable information. We can conclude that Company A has a retention problem, and it's getting worse. Three years ago, the industry average was 6 years, and Company A was 5.5 years. Then the Company A tenure duration went down each year, while the industry average stayed the same.

The question is, why are Company A employees jumping ship faster than their peers in other companies? Can this trend be reversed?

The impulsive CEO might say, "Make our employees sign nondisclosure agreements. And offer them a two percent raise. That should take care of the problem!"

Such a response is guaranteed to miss the mark. It might even make the problem worse.

What's needed is a comprehensive, organization-wide effort to drill down and identify why Company A employees are expressing their unhappiness by quitting sooner than others. It could be the pay structure. It could be the lack of promotion paths. It could be a toxic work environment, or dehumanizing practices. It could be the average age of the customer is getting older, which suggests to employees that the company is in slow decline.

When you have solid information, aggregate and organize your insights into a presentation that you use to collaborate with a greater team to get validation and additional fine-tuning elements. This is an important step because it gives stakeholders the opportunity to agree upon the current state of happiness.

4. Organize

In the first three steps, you (1) made the decision to get serious about your happy workplace, (2) gathered data about the current level of stakeholder happiness in your organization, and (3) turned that raw data into action-able information. You now know what you need to achieve and you've tar-geted some specific areas that demand improvement. These areas could be directly related to employee happiness or they could focus more on cus-tomer happiness, such as the earlier example of the hospital waiting room. In that case, improving patient happiness would also improve the happiness of the intake staff. A secondary effect can be just as good as a primary effect.

Your company comprises people, from a handful in one location to many thousands across the globe. Call them moving parts, if you will. As the leader—of your division or the entire company—your job is to direct the activities of your people to produce value for your customers, your stakeholders, and your investors.

In a small firm, you can take a hands-on approach and lead the effort yourself. But it's more likely that you'll need to work through the managers who report to you. They are your ambassadors to your many employees and stakeholders. They represent you.

Either way, it's up to you to not only specify what you want, but also *model what you want.*

There is no other way to do it. If you want a happy workplace, you must set the example. Remember, we're talking about human emotion. You cannot command people to be happy. You can tell them what task to perform, or when to take a lunch break, or where to sit in the office, but you cannot tell them to be happy.

Happiness is contagious. It's been scientifically proven. A study by researchers at Harvard Medical School and the University of California of nearly 5,000 individuals over a period of twenty years found that when an individual becomes happy, the network effect can be measured up to three degrees. That is, one person's happiness triggers a chain reaction that benefits not only his immediate friends, but also their friends and their friends' friends.[3]

"Everyday interactions we have with other people are definitely contagious, in terms of happiness," said Nicholas Christakis, a professor at Harvard Medical School and an author of the study, to *Harvard Medicine*. "Rather than asking how we can get happier, we should be asking how we can increase happiness all around us. When you make positive changes in your own life, those effects ripple out from you and you can find yourself surrounded by the very thing you fostered."[4]

Construct a happiness team that will work as the happiness leaders to build out the formal happiness strategy. Building out the strategy will consist of tools such as happiness hackathons, personification development, journey mapping, happiness baseline and improvement measurements, and other standard aspects of a strategic initiative.

You should also have a project manager on your team who manages the collection and organization of the disparate components in a way that manages time and optimizes results. When you do this, you'll be in good company. Top firms including Google, Salesforce, Airbnb, Zappos, Charity Water, and Chefs Club have created positions specifically dedicated to maintaining and improving employees' experience and company culture. These executives have various titles including chief happiness officer (CHO), head of employee experience, or vice president of global employee success. Their job is to manage the strategy and processes related to boosting and maintaining the overall level of employee happiness and the resulting rise in productivity and customer satisfaction. They influence any and all people-centered activities, including hiring, training, performance management, professional development, and recognition while ensuring the company's growth and bottom line show positive results.

Your CHO must have robust institutional support. Because the CHO needs to work across departmental lines, and therefore must invade the "turf" of other managers, three minimums are required.

1. The CHO must have clearly delineated authority granted to him or her by the CEO. While this authority won't include the ability to hire and fire outside his or her own department,

it must include the ability to summon employees for special training sessions, for example.

2. The other managers must be told the CHO has authority in certain areas. This message or memo must come from the CEO.
3. The CHO must have a budget. Even if it's relatively small, the budget must be real and it must be carefully targeted.

The CHO cannot do it alone, just like the CEO can't do it alone either. It's up to each and every member of the organization, from the board of directors to individual employees, to make an effort and actively participate in creating a happy workplace.

5. Launch Your Happiness as a Strategy Initiative

It's important to launch a happy initiative only after you are absolutely certain that you have an airtight strategy that includes the budget, time, leadership commitment, communication strategy, and all of the other elements that are required to make happiness at work a reality. You should also leverage internal enterprise social networks to create ongoing dialogue across stakeholders and departments. The best organizations use happiness challenges as a way to get great ideas that turn into great innovations and ultimately a happy workforce.

Your Happiness as a Strategy (HaaS) plan needs to be real and written down. It can be as short as a few bullet points or as long as a multifaceted text with graphics that analyzes happiness and discusses building your happiness brand. It should gain insights across all stakeholders by building a strategic framework and cross-functional team architecture, and by creating a communication strategy, survey design, effective project management, budgeting, events, and reporting. Each organization will create their own unique architecture of elements for their strategy. The most important thing to keep in mind is that your initiative has to be complete prior to launching it.

For specific insights into the components of your HaaS plan, let's go back to the definition of workplace happiness:

"The engagement of purposeful work that serves our personal growth, in a way that positively impacts and serves others."

You, the employer and leader, can boost happiness in these three areas:

1. **Purposeful work.** Here, you can ensure that the actual work being done by your employees is not boring or demeaning. However, a CEO might point out that this is often easier said than done, because work often requires repetitive tasks. Not every job is exciting!

   There are two ways to respond to this.

   The first is to ensure that each employee knows how his or her job contributes to the success of the group. The easiest way to do this is to thank them for a job well done—not at the end of the year, but at the end of every day.

   The second way is to create a system of cross-training, whereby employees are exposed to the work done by others. The benefits of cross-training are well known and significant. It helps ensure that if an essential team member quits or takes a vacation, another worker can cover for them and the business won't suffer. It creates a more agile workforce that's better equipped to handle transitions gracefully and recover quickly from disruptions. This means you can deliver seamless service to your customers, even in times of turmoil.

   The work itself can be broken up into more appealing chunks. At Adobe Inc., which has been named the happiest workplace in the United States, Gloria Chen, the company's chief people officer, told CNBC the company responded to the Covid-19 pandemic by measuring employee sentiment through surveys, hosting company all-hands meetings and focus groups to better understand the challenges of working through the pandemic, and proposing solutions to maintain employee happiness.

In response to employee feedback, the company introduced flexible work schedules to accommodate caregiving responsibilities, monthly companywide days off, 20 new paid days off each year for employees "directly impacted by significant events like pandemics or natural disasters," and an increase of its wellness reimbursement to $600 per year.[5]

Adobe couldn't stop the pandemic, but they could respond to it.

2. **Personal growth.** As a leader, you're probably facing new challenges every day, and perhaps even every hour! You need to be a "jack of all trades," and the learning curve is steep. The same might be true for employees working in R&D, as they're constantly trying new ideas. Therefore, personal growth may not be an issue for you. But you might forget that many of your employees are doing the same thing, day after day. Every business relies on systems, which by definition are repetitive. This might be necessary, but a lack of personal growth can kill happiness very quickly. Your HaaS plan needs to include ways to keep your employees challenged. One of the best is to have a policy of promoting from within, so that employees know they have a shot at moving up the ladder. You can support continuing education programs and pay for employees to take courses. Reward innovative ideas from any and every part of the business, and make sure your employees know the company seeks and values their new ideas.

3. **Positively impacts others.** If you're a front-line salesperson, it's easy to see how your product or service impacts the customer. But if your job keeps you buried somewhere deep in the supply chain, it can be difficult to see how moving a pallet of parts from one warehouse to another impacts anyone's life. This is why every employee must be aware of the overall mission of the organization and see how their effort helps the organization fulfill it.

    Create or support a program whereby employees are encouraged to volunteer their time—on the company clock—with a local charitable organization. This means that even if all employees don't see how their product or service directly impacts their customers, at least they can have the sense that the brand is being a good neighbor and helping improve the community.

This brings us to the idea that while the everyday job of every employee may not be terribly exciting, if the employees know that the organization *in general* is dedicated to doing good things, that will boost their level of happiness.

6. Monitor, Measure, and Fix

Happy cultures are dynamic and fluid, and there is no way to create a successful initiative without eliminating the elements that aren't working well and reinvesting in those elements that do work. Conduct ongoing real rating surveys, happiness hackathons, and listening sessions to continue to improve upon the bold mission of improving the quality life of your employees.

Go back to Step 2: Listen, Learn, and Collaborate. You should have a system for replicating this step on an ongoing basis. Your RealRatings survey is just one tool in your box. Additional strategies may include:

1. **Just ask them!** Keep it simple and just ask. As the CEO, you come into contact with many subordinates during the day. When you see one, you can say, "How are you today? Is there any particular problem I can help you with?" This is the essence of servant leadership. When subordinates believe their only role is to "get results or get out," the last thing they'll do is confide in you that they've got a difficult problem. They'll tough it out until failure crushes them. To avoid this, create a safe environment for team members to give you feedback at any time. Treat your employees like team members and you're the coach.

2. **Encourage initiative and innovation.** If your employees are doing only what they're told, then you have a stale

environment without any creative energy. If they're spearheading new projects, finding new solutions for problems, and adding new elements to their positions, then you have a winning company culture. Productivity and well-being build a resilient, engaged, and hardworking workforce and help attract and retain your top talent.

Innovation hackathons are events in which any employee can participate. In the old days, they called them "brainstorming sessions." Same thing. You sit around and toss out ideas. The only rule is this: No idea is too far-fetched or crazy. Bring it out! The good ideas will rise to the surface.

3. **Track late arrivals.** It may sound simplistic, but keeping an eye on employee tardiness can reveal how employees feel about their work and are coping with their responsibilities. Being late for work can signify many things, but if it's consistent, then the employee may be struggling with their work/life balance or finding ways to delay coming to work, or have issues with kids getting to school. Finding out the reason can often clear the air and lead to greater employee happiness. The best way to know if an employee is truly happy with you is by checking the consistency of an employee's attitude, performance, and attendance.

4. **Assign a new task.** Periodically ask an employee to do something that takes them out of their comfort zone. (Be sure you provide them sufficient time to do it. Otherwise, the employee will feel as though you're squeezing them for extra work!) If your request is met with enthusiasm, you have a happy employee who is motivated to grow with your company. If you are met with foot-dragging, then the employee is most likely unhappy and disengaged, or feels anxiety about their position.

5. **Monitor Glassdoor, Indeed, Fairygodboss, Vault, and other employer review websites.** It's no fun to read the negative reviews of your company online! And yes, a certain percentage of negative reviews are posted by the classic

"disgruntled employee" who hates everything and everyone, and whom you will never please. And while a specific complaint might grab your attention, it's useful to look at the overall trends. These sites will rank your business against others in your industry, and you'll see what prospective employees will see when they check out your company profile. They'll see similar companies doing similar work, and which of the bunch receive the best overall ratings from current and past employees.

Measure the changes in the happiness of your employees. Hopefully, by the metrics you've chosen, you'll see it going up!

7. Celebrate

Last but certainly not least, it's incredibly important that you celebrate the innovators who create great ideas that go into implementation. It's also important to constantly communicate and celebrate the benefits that are being realized in order to maintain the momentum of your happiness initiative. Be sure that while you may shine a spotlight on a particular "employee of the month" or a department's outstanding performance, everyone in your company knows that it's a team effort, and one employee's winning month is a win for everyone.

You might even want to follow in the footsteps of Gary Bertch, who cofounded Bertch Cabinets with his wife in 1977. In 2016, the Waterloo, Iowa, company took all 800 of its employees on a weeklong cruise through the Caribbean. Bertch had offered the trip as incentive to employees the previous year. When they met their goals, he came through with his promise. The luxury Carnival Cruise liner took employees around the Caribbean, including a stop in Cozumel, Mexico.

"We just tried to get all of our people pumped up a little more to achieve the various goals, both customer-oriented goals and financial goals," Bertch told the *Waterloo-Cedar Falls Courier*.

And if an employee couldn't go? Bertch offered a cash bonus option for those unable to travel (or in need of the extra money). And everyone got the week off. "It's terrific," he told NBC's *Today* show. "Everyone works hard for a common effort and reaps the rewards. I'm just looking forward to seeing all of our associates enjoying themselves."[6]

That's the bottom line. If you're going to ask your employees to spend a significant part of their lives working for your company, then why not make them happy to do so? You'll receive better work as a result, which will lead to greater long-term success.

Take Action!

✓ With this Happiness Ecosystem action plan, you can transform your organization from miserable (at worst) or merely average (better, but not good enough!) to truly extraordinary and super-competitive. Here are the steps:

1. **Define happiness.** For our purposes, here's how I define happiness on the job: "The engagement of purposeful work that serves our personal growth, in a way that positively impacts and serves others."

2. **Listen, learn, and collaborate.** In order to know what you want to become, you have to know your current condition. You need to cast aside your preconceptions and biases, and get a grip on the state of your organization. The energy flow is in all directions, and as CEO, your job is to manage this energy flow to produce the highest level of stakeholder happiness possible.

3. **Validate.** Data must be turned into actionable information. Aggregate and organize your insights into a presentation that you use to collaborate with a greater team to get buy-in and additional fine-tuning elements.

4. **Organize.** Your job is to direct the activities of your people to produce happiness for your customers, your stakeholders, and your investors. Assemble a happiness team to build out the formal happiness strategy. You might even appoint a chief happiness officer (CHO), head of employee experience, or vice president of global employee success.

5. **Launch your happiness as a strategy (HaaS) plan.** It needs to be real and written down and complete prior to launching it. It must activate the three key areas: "The engagement of purposeful work (1) that serves our personal growth (2), in a way that positively impacts and serves others (3)."

6. **Monitor, measure, and fix.** Happy cultures are dynamic and fluid, and you must continually eliminate the elements that aren't working well and reinvest in those elements that do work.

7. **Celebrate.** It's important that you celebrate the innovators while ensuring everyone in your company knows that it's a team effort, and one employee's victory is a win for everyone.

Thank You for Reading

Thank you for reading *Happy Work*. The intention of this book is to challenge the framework and beliefs of the traditional company culture "best practice." Getting out of your comfort zone and taking a fresh look at the happiness of your employees requires courage and a willingness to be open to new ideas. The principles revealed on these pages are based on a lifetime of study and hands-on experience working shoulder to shoulder with leaders and employees alike, and they've been used in my own practice with significant success across multiple industries and organizations. I trust that your application of these practical solutions will serve you and your organization well.

My most sincere thanks—and I wish you every success!

Notes

Chapter 1

1. CNBC. https://www.cnbc.com/2019/02/25/warren-buffett-plays-bridge-8-hours-a-week-and-can-beat-bill-gates.html
2. US Army. https://www.goarmy.com/benefits/money/basic-pay-active-duty-soldiers.html
3. https://www.careerbliss.com/walmart/salaries/
4. https://www.businessinsider.com/amazon-employee-salary-pay-median-worker-compensation-compared-jeff-bezos-2021-4
5. US Army. https://www.army.mil/article/243986/after_challenging_year_army_posts_high_marks_in_civilian_employee_survey
6. https://www.wearethemighty.com/popular/army-job-best-according-glassdoor/
7. USArmy. https://www.army.mil/article/223295/army_retention_hits_goal_five_months_early
8. *New York Times.* https://www.nytimes.com/1970/09/13/archives/a-friedman-doctrine-the-social-responsibility-of-business-is-to.html

Chapter 2

1. https://www.macmillanhighered.com/BrainHoney/Resource/6696/digital_first_content/trunk/test/hewittlawson2e/hewittlawson2e_docs17_6.html
2. Entrepreneur.com. https://www.entrepreneur.com/article/381850
3. US Dept Labor. https://www.bls.gov/news.release/jolts.t04.htm
4. BBC. https://www.bbc.com/worklife/article/20210629-the-great-resignation-how-employers-drove-workers-to-quit

5. HBR. https://hbr.org/resources/pdfs/comm/achievers/hbr_achievers_report_sep13.pdf
6. Brent Hamer et al. https://pubmed.ncbi.nlm.nih.gov/25851184/#affiliation-1
7. iOpener Institute. https://insights.iopenerinstitute.com/insights/an-iopener-case-study
8. Warwick.ac.uk. https://warwick.ac.uk/newsandevents/pressreleases/new_study_shows/
9. SHRM. https://lrshrm.shrm.org/blog/2017/10/essential-elements-employee-retention

Chapter 3

1. PayScale. https://www.payscale.com/data-packages/employee-loyalty/least-loyal-employees
2. https://www.businessinsider.com/companies-ranked-by-turnover-rates-2013-7
3. CNBC. https://www.cnbc.com/2018/05/07/what-working-at-mcdonalds-taught-jay-leno-about-success.html
4. https://www.republictimes.net/longtime-school-custodian-retires/
5. Glassdoor. https://www.glassdoor.com/about-us/glassdoor-survey-finds-americans-forfeit-earned-vacationpaid-time/
6. Inc.com. https://www.inc.com/heather-r-huhman/these-companies-dropped-traditional-employee-feedback-surveys-havent-looked-back-you-should-too.html
7. https://www.globenewswire.com/en/news-release/2020/08/28/2085261/28124/en/10-Billion-Worldwide-Online-Survey-Software-Industry-to-2025-Retail-is-Widely-Using-Online-Survey-Software-for-Understanding-Consumer-Behavior.html
8. https://www.knowledge-sourcing.com/report/global-online-survey-software-market

Chapter 4

1. https://www.weforum.org/reports/gender-gap-2020-report-100-years-pay-equality/digest
2. New York Times. https://www.nytimes.com/2020/09/26/world/covid-women-childcare-equality.html
3. HBR. https://hbr.org/2018/05/what-most-people-get-wrong-about-men-and-women

Chapter 5

1. https://www.restaurantdive.com/news/mcdonalds-investor-sues-chain-for
   -handling-of-easterbrook-exit/604124/

Chapter 6

1. https://www.northwestern.edu/hr/about/news/february-2019/the-cost-of-a
   -bad-hire.html
2. SHRM. https://www.shrm.org/resourcesandtools/hr-topics/employee
   -relations/pages/cost-of-bad-hires.aspx
3. https://blog.hubspot.com/blog/tabid/6307/bid/33749/7-companies-that
   -totally-get-their-buyer-personas.aspx
4. *New York Times*. https://www.nytimes.com/2009/07/19/automobiles/
   19design.html
5. 29 CFR § 1608.3

Chapter 7

1. WAPO. https://www.washingtonpost.com/wp-dyn/articles/A45322-2004
   Aug29_2.html
2. HopkinsMedicine.org. https://www.hopkinsmedicine.org/news/media/
   releases/burned_out_depressed_surgeons_more_likely_to_commit_more_
   major_medical_errors
3. AMA. https://www.ama-assn.org/practice-management/physician-health/
   half-health-workers-report-burnout-amid-covid-19
4. U.C. https://facilities.uchicago.edu/about/mission/

Chapter 8

1. https://arabesque.com/research/From_the_stockholder_to_the_stakeholder
   _web.pdf
2. Patagonia. https://www.patagonia.com/stories/benefit-corporation-update
   -patagonia-passes-b-impact-assessment-improves-score-to-116/story-17871
   .html
3. Glassdoor. https://www.glassdoor.com/Reviews/Patagonia-Reviews-E5474.htm
4. B Lab. https://bcorporation.net/node/39533
5. https://www.zenbusiness.com/blog/most-valuable-b-corps/
6. Dr. Bronner. https://www.drbronner.com/about/
7. Beneficial State Bank. https://beneficialstatebank.com/our-story/join-our
   -team

8. Glassdoor. https://www.glassdoor.com/Overview/Working-at-Beneficial -State-Bank-EI_IE995526.11,32.htm

Chapter 9

1. HBR. https://hbr.org/2018/03/research-how-one-bad-employee-can -corrupt-a-whole-team
2. Felps, Mitchell, Byington. https://s3-us-west-2.amazonaws.com/oww-files -public/a/a5/Final_BA_ROB.pdf
3. CNBC. https://www.cnbc.com/2021/09/15/in-2020-top-ceos-earned-351 -times-more-than-the-typical-worker.html
4. Comparably. https://www.comparably.com/awards/winners/happiness -2021-large
5. Adobe. https://blog.adobe.com/en/publish/2021/02/09/forbes-award -americas-best-employers#gs.gw63m2
6. Forbes. https://www.forbes.com/best-large-employers/#5c472b86fb3e
7. Fortune. https://fortune.com/worlds-best-workplaces/2021/adobe-systems/
8. People. https://people.com/human-interest/people-100-companies-that -care-2021/?slide=c02513ab-506d-44fa-9560-6876763be0aa#c02513ab -506d-44fa-9560-6876763be0aa

Chapter 10

1. HP.com. https://press.hp.com/content/dam/sites/garage-press/press/press -kits/2020/2020-innovation-summit/hp_wes_infographic.pdf
2. Deloitte. https://www2.deloitte.com/us/en/insights/focus/technology-and -the-future-of-work/intelligent-automation-2020-survey-results.html
3. UOIT. https://shared.uoit.ca/shared/faculty-sites/sustainability-today/ publications/population-predictions-of-the-101-largest-cities-in-the-55t 7 -century.pdf?__hstc=132141777.2e4c626 6acf0a2cfe301206fbac36b83 .1637705832649.1637705832649 .1637705832649.1&__hssc=13214177 7.1.1637705832650&__hsfp=791940003
4. Inc. https://www.inc.com/gabrielle-bienasz/ecommerce-online-retail -amazon-walmart-digital-commerce-360-report-2020.html
5. Statista. https://www.statista.com/statistics/266282/annual-net-revenue-of -amazoncom/
6. Owl Labs. https://resources.owllabs.com/state-of-remote-work/2019
7. Microsoft. https://www.microsoft.com/en-gb/business/work-smarter-to -live-better/

8. TechRepublic. https://www.techrepublic.com/article/remote-workers-say -theyre-happier-but-working-from-home-brings-its-own-problems/
9. *Miami Herald*. https://www.miamiherald.com/news/coronavirus/ article246510310.html
10. *Miami Herald*. https://www.miamiherald.com/news/coronavirus/ article246510310.html
11. Yahoo. https://www.yahoo.com/now/17-worst-companies-america -170000191.html
12. UP. https://www.up.com/aboutup/esg/building-america-report/index.htm
13. Indeed.com. https://www.indeed.com/cmp/Union-Pacific/reviews
14. Indeed.com. https://www.indeed.com/cmp/Norfolk-Southern-Corp/reviews
15. Glassdoor.com. https://www.glassdoor.com/Reviews/Norfolk-Southern -Reviews-E483.htm
16. Glassdoor.com. https://www.glassdoor.com/Reviews/BNSF-Railway -Reviews-E18514.htm

Chapter 11

1. DailyDot. https://www.dailydot.com/debug/amazon-workers-told-not-to -pack-up-early-tiktok/
2. Zippia.com. https://www.zippia.com/advice/cost-of-hiring-statistics -average-cost-per-hire/
3. AMA. https://www.amanet.org/articles/why-zappos-com-pays-new-hires-1 -000-to-quit/
4. CNBC. https://www.cnbc.com/2018/05/21/why-amazon-pays-employees -5000-to-quit.html
5. SHRM. https://www.shrm.org/resourcesandtools/hr-topics/employee -relations/pages/retirees-return-to-work-.aspx
6. ResumeBuilder. https://www.resumebuilder.com/labor-shortages-driving -demand-for-retirees/
7. SHRM. https://www.shrm.org/resourcesandtools/hr-topics/employee -relations/pages/retirees-return-to-work-.aspx

Chapter 13

1. McMahon. https://www.amazon.com/Happiness-History-Darrin-M -McMahon/dp/0802142893
2. Davis, Tchiki. https://www.berkeleywellbeing.com/what-is-happiness.html
3. BMJ. https://www.bmj.com/content/337/bmj.a2338

4. https://hms.harvard.edu/magazine/science-emotion/contagion-happiness
5. CNBC. https://www.cnbc.com/2021/10/06/comparably-top-10
-companies-with-the-happiest-employees-in-2021.html
6. NBC Today. https://www.today.com/kindness/best-boss-ever-bertch
-cabinets-takes-staff-800-caribbean-cruise-t106542

About Nicholas J. Webb

Nicholas J. Webb is one of the top company culture experts in the world. He has been awarded the Global Gurus Top 30 designation for customer service for seven years in a row. Nick is the CEO of myLearnLogic.com, an employee and company culture training and advisory firm that works with some of the top brands to help them build world-class employee and customer experiences.

As a technologist, he has been awarded more than forty US patents for consumer and technology products. He has also served as an adjunct professor for a health science university, where he led the Center for Innovation.

Nick is the author of multiple number one best-selling books in the areas of business innovation, customer and employee experience, and leadership. He is also one of the top keynote speakers in the areas of business growth, innovation, future trends, and company culture.

Learn More About How Nick
Can Help Your Organization

Nick is always excited to learn about how his readers have applied his methods to drive world-class employee and customer experience in their own organizations. He can be contacted through his consulting and training firm at www.goleaderlogic.com, or for speaking engagements at www.nickwebb.com.

Business leaders access Nick's growing portfolio of services through these five online platforms:

LearnLogic

LearnLogic offers a wide range of online learning opportunities to help leaders optimize their workforce while giving them the skills they need to drive enterprise excellence. Our goal is to create and deliver the highest quality training programs that serve both our students and the organizations they work for.

We make building a happy work culture fast and predictable. We begin with a Cultural Readiness Assessment (CRA) to determine your current state of work life. Then, we build out a world-class Strategy, with measurements that will rapidly move the happiness needle in your organization. Lastly, we develop a customized Certification Training Program for your leadership and teams. It's just that easy!

Our Happiness Certified™ program will significantly improve the quality of work-life for your employees while also improving customer experience. The benefits to an organization include increased productivity, higher Glassdoor ratings, significant improvements in customer satisfaction, retention, and promotion, and the ability to attract and keep the best talent.

Find out more at www.mylearnlogic.com.

The Happy Thought Club Podcast

Building organizational growth through happy employees and customers is a dynamic process that requires continuous study and insights. With that in mind, Nick has created a podcast that provides quick and easy insights for his readers to keep their happy culture going strong.

To learn more about Nick's podcast, visit his podcast site at www.thehappythoughtclub.com.

RealRatings

Simply stated, we're in the happiness business. We help organizations drive enterprise growth and returns on strategy through happy employees and customers. We do this with one of the best knowledge bases in the industry and proven systems that deliver an exceptional return on our client's investment, and we guarantee it.

We deliver major improvements in productivity, presentism, and FTE yield; help you attract and retain valuable mission-critical talent; boost return on strategy, innovation, and customer satisfaction; and much more.

Learn more at www.myrealratings.com.

LeaderLogic and Happiness as a Strategy (HaaS) Consulting

We work with great organizations and their leaders to help them develop the skills and competencies they need to lead complex and diverse teams. We provide strategies, advisory services, and training to help leaders drive sustainable and scalable growth, and make significant improvements on strategic initiatives. We do this with a thoughtful and handcrafted approach that delivers predictable and significant returns on our client's investment.

Despite the fact they are widely used, traditional employee surveys often provide erroneous and non-actionable data. This is precisely why most organizations are not able to move the needle on employee happiness. Employee happiness requires improved listening, ideation, and a wide range of other methods to get the real insights to drive meaningful and measurable change. That's what we do.

For more information, please visit www.goleaderlogic.com.

Keynote Speaking, Workshops, and Events

Nick is listed and booked by the top speaker bureaus in the world as a keynote speaker for mission-critical events hosted by top brands. Nicholas routinely receives a five-star rating for his customized talks that take an entertaining and fun approach to delivering actionable content. Nick books out each year and has a reach of tens of thousands of happy audience members.

He inspires and challenges global audiences with keynote presentations in Virtual Events, Innovation, Healthcare, Customer Experience, Future Trends, and Leadership and Worklife. He'll leave your people ready to create a bright future for themselves and their community.

For more information, please visit www.nickwebb.com.